The Anarchist Revelation

Being What We're Meant To Be

Paul Cudenec

For B & J and an end to separation

Published by Winter Oak Press, Sussex, England

winteroak@greenmail.net

ISBN: 978-0-9576566-0-4

CONTENTS

Preface   **vii**

I   A World Gone Mad   **1**

II   Freedom Obstructed   **13**

III   Dump the System!   **27**

IV   The Lie of Democracy   **39**

V   Anarchy Is Life   **53**

VI   The Courage to Exist   **63**

VII   Our Spirit Is Universal!   **73**

VIII   Cleansing Fires of Revolution   **89**

IX   The Anarchist Paradox   **101**

X   The Poetry of Revolt   **111**

XI   ¡Viva La Revelación!   **121**

Endnotes   **127**

PREFACE

There are a few things that need clarifying about the text that follows. Firstly, I should stress that in quoting any writer, I am in no way endorsing anything else they may have said or written elsewhere. For instance, as this book was being prepared for publication, Derrick Jensen was being reported as expressing views with which I would not want to be associated, much though I have so far admired his work.

Secondly, much of the emphasis here is on individuals and the way in which we can clear our minds of all the detritus of the ego in order to be true to ourselves. However, this is not to say that the message is an individualist one, as a certain comrade felt it was, having read a draft. The reason why individuals must follow this path is so that they can better channel and carry out the needs of the larger whole. It's amusing that in a previous essay, *Antibodies*, the same idea was approached from a different angle and led to the occasional accusation that here individuality was being rejected outright in favour of a collective identity! The point is that individual self-realisation and collective solidarity are two aspects of the same thing. The lack of either one leads to the loss of the other.

The second critical observation made was that not all anarchists are "outsiders" and endure an alienation from society as described. Yes, of course, plenty of anarchists flourish in welcoming social circles and communities and, as active people, are perhaps less likely to exist in a state of personal isolation than others. However, the discovery of like-minded people with whom one can share a life usually comes as a result of an initial alienation and the seeking-out of a reality other than the one prescribed by society as a whole. The anarchist vision is so profoundly at odds with everything on which our current society is based – all that domination, exploitation and control enforced by state-sanctioned violence – that it is not possible to be an anarchist and *not* feel alienated from that world and the mindset that uncritically accepts it. There may be those who are happy to label themselves "anarchists" for superficial reasons, without ever fully understanding the gulf between their outlook and that imposed by the status quo, but if they are to integrate the label with their inner identity, they will have to accept the enormity of the divide and go through the resulting self-realisation.

There is also an intermediate stage, in which many of us will have found ourselves floundering, where we understand the situation rationally but have not absorbed it emotionally. We still cling to certain insecurities and vanities that are part of the very way of being which we reject. Human communities in which there are no petty personality clashes or pointless disputes will probably never exist, but the frequency with which they occur will be reduced in proportion to the number of those who undergo the soul-searching and inner purification recommended by humanity's universal inherited wisdom.

Being an "outsider" is thus a stage in a personal transformation which we must all experience if we are ever to emerge from the perpetual self-obsessed adolescence encouraged by contemporary society. Whether this change is sudden or gradual, pleasant or painful, whether it occurs during youth, adulthood or even old age, will vary between individuals. But if we are to align our inner selves with the strength and clarity of the cause we embrace, and thus allow ourselves to offer up our full unoccluded potential, it is a process that no anarchist would want to avoid.

As far as the rest of the content of the essay goes, that can safely be left to speak for itself.

"He who knows both knowledge and action, with action overcomes death and with knowledge reaches immortality"

Isa Upanishad, Bhagavad Gita

I

A WORLD GONE MAD

It is almost impossible to lead a truly meaningful life in the modern world. However hard we try to distract ourselves, we cannot shake off a profound and uneasy sense of dislocation, emptiness and loss. Is this all there is? Is this who I really am? How can I feel more deeply? How can I feel more real? How can I feel more alive? We thrash about all over the place looking for reasons and solutions, but all too often follow false trails, discover partial causes and ways of thinking that offer merely temporary respite or, even worse, time-wasting distraction from the core problem.

Sometimes we even doubt our own sanity and wonder whether the fault does not lie entirely in our own heads, before our reading, conversations and life experiences remind us of what Herbert Marcuse refers to as "Freud's fundamental insight that the patient's trouble is rooted in a *general* sickness which cannot be cured by analytic therapy"[1] and of Derrick Jensen's conviction that "the culture as a whole and most of its members are insane".[2] So we turn back to try and work out what exactly has gone wrong with our world, but the task has become no easier. Where do we start? The question is as difficult in the context of these written words as it is for the individual in private contemplation, but one way of trying to reveal the essence of the problem is to begin with one of the many ways in which it manifests itself and then travel deeper.

For instance, we might look at the early twenty-first century obsession with electronic communication – people constantly bent over the latest device, frantically scrolling, texting and updating – and conclude that they are suffering from some kind of addictive disorder, an overwhelming need for constant connection with a "social" network in which the frequency and number of contacts seems to have replaced any need for depth or content. As François Brune notes, we no longer have the right to "what you could call creative solitude" – the dizzy pleasures of technologies like the mobile phone preventing the individual from existing by him or herself.[3]

We might then go on to acknowledge that this is merely the latest development in a long process of alienation through technology and that possibly worse crimes against the human spirit have been committed by an insidiously passive and near-universal activity in which communication is purely one-way. Television is, says Jean-Jacques Wunenburger, the confiscation of life.[4] We are no longer ourselves when we watch the screen, adds Guillaume Carnino, but instead our consciousness is flattened into the play of images and "we become what we watch".[5] Television is a way of escaping from our own thoughts, our own selves,[6] he says. Escaping from our thoughts or being prevented from having them? Whatever the illusion of choice, television-watching is not something that any of us elect to do on an individual basis – it has become part of a so-called culture to which we belong by default from birth and from which we have to positively opt out, if we so choose.

Here we begin to reach beyond the symptoms and towards the underlying causes of our social sickness. There is no room in our world for real individuality, individuality that emerges from the depths of the soul, but only for the quasi-individuality of increasingly complex but nevertheless severely limited "lifestyle" choices. Capitalist consumer society denies our very integrity – not only as individuals but, by extension, as a society. It creates the empty neediness of dislocated existences and then proposes "solutions" from its own stockrooms. It seeks to persuade us that the way to rid ourselves of that gnawing despair is to comfort or distract ourselves by means of more and more material possessions and, at the same time, to blind ourselves to what we are doing by accepting the suggestion that we either need or deserve whatever it is that we are buying. It denies us the chance to sink the roots of our own unique identities and then tries to sell us the constituent parts of an artificial consumer "personality" to differentiate ourselves from all the other lost and lonely souls.

The result is that we live surrounded by people with fake identities, in a brittle plastic palace where, as Joseph Campbell puts it, "men who are fractions imagine themselves to be complete".[7] Jean Baudrillard and others have pointed out the central role played by the smoke and mirrors of advertising in conjuring up all these phoney "needs" that industrial society claims to fill (thus justifying its existence and the "necessity" of its continuation) – not just in its most obvious and direct form but through the use of the mass media to construct around us a pseudo-reality in order to restrict our consciousness and channel it in the directions required. It is not simply an unfortunate *by-product* of this situation that most people seem unhappy – on the contrary, persuading people that they are *not content* with themselves or their lives is, as Aldous Huxley observes, the primary aim of this mental manipulation: "Spoken or printed, broadcast over the ether or on wood-pulp, all advertising copy has but one purpose – to prevent the will from ever achieving silence. Desirelessness is the condition of deliverance and illumination. The condition of an expanding and technologically progressive system of mass-production is universal craving. Advertising is the organized effort to extend and intensify craving..."[8]

There is something deeply disturbing about the clinical ruthlessness with which the commercial system attacks people's minds in order to turn them into malleable consumer-robots. In their 2012 study of advertising (which focuses particularly on issues around gender), Sophie Pietrucci, Chris Vientiane and Aude Vincent cite a revealing admission made by Patrick Le Lay, head of France's main TV channel, TF1, to *Le Monde* newspaper in which he describes the role of his programmes as making the viewer's mind *disponible* (receptive) – "that's to say to entertain and relax it so it becomes prepared between two advertisements. What we are selling to Coca-Cola is time with a receptive human brain".[9] It's worth pondering on this insight, which obviously applies to other TV channels in other countries. The advertisements may seem like interruptions to the entertainment being provided – perhaps we imagine that they are merely required to pay for the programmes – but in fact they are the whole *raison d'être* of the channel and its entire output. The whole thing is just one, endless advertisement – produced with sufficient sophistication to ensure this is not obvious to the average viewer (and if non-commercial state TV does not operate in quite the same way, we may wonder whether its doses of entertainment merely make the viewers' brains receptive to the state-authorised values and assumptions promoted in the "news").

The power of advertising has become almost absolute as it hones its techniques and gains control over more of our everyday experiences, creating a perception of ourselves and the outside world which is completely at odds with reality. How can it be, for instance, that it has persuaded fresh-faced teenage girls to use moisturiser and other "beauty" products designed to delay or disguise the effects of ageing in much older women? Why is it that so many people accept that the simplest of activities – taking a walk in the countryside, for instance – must necessarily involve paying for specialist clothing or accessories? How is it that shopping has become a hobby, that the purchase of objects is equated in so many minds with a sense of achievement or satisfaction? The extent of advertising's influence over society is such that Brune, for one, regards it as "totalitarian" – the difference from previous forms of totalitarianism being that it is less brutal but a lot more insidious. He recalls Huxley's comment that the key to social stability is to make people want exactly what you've got lined up for them anyway, which is precisely what advertising sets out to do.[10] The goods come first, then the "need", in the same way that politicians devise new legislation behind closed doors before developing, with the connivance of the media, news storylines that lead the public to clamour for – or at least go along with – the very action that had always secretly been planned.

There's a falsity here, which pervades everything we do. Things are never what they seem to be. We are rapidly losing touch with truth and have been for some time. Gustav Landauer is already complaining in 1911: "Progress, what you call progress, this incessant hustle-bustle, this rapid tiring and neurasthenic, short-breathed chase after novelty, after anything new as long as it is new, this progress and the crazy ideas of the practitioners of development associated with it... this progress, this unsteady, restless haste; this inability to remain still and this perpetual desire to be on the move, this so-called progress is a symptom of our abnormal condition, our unculture".[11]

In our society there are always intermediaries between our personal experience and reality. Most of us buy our food from shops – we don't see vegetables grown or animals raised and slaughtered. We spend our lives performing tasks that can seem pointless except in terms of indirectly providing us with the means to live. We arrange our existences around money as if it was something real. The possessions in which we invest so much value, from cars to washing machines, are, as scientist and writer Kit Pedler sees, "symbols of despair and failure: surrogates for achievement, which encourage us to live on the outside of our senses and actually diminish the quality of life".[12] Carnino points out that "having, and no longer being, is the sole source of our desire,"[13] and there is a horrible sense of us having abandoned our own selves, our own destinies, under the hypnosis of mass exploitation.

At the heart of the modern sickness is the loss of a true sense of identity. We don't know who we are and we don't know who we're meant to be or what we're meant to be doing with our brief lives. We can't touch or even see our own sense of meaning because it is hidden behind the walls of a prison that has been built – that we ourselves have collectively built – around us. Needless to say, this loss is also reflected in our culture, or "unculture" as Landauer has it. With no notion of any meaning, no connection to the depths of our being, our arts are too often focused on empty form, imitation or ugly caricature.

Both Baudrillard[14] and the English anarchist Herbert Read were depressed by the emergence of Pop Art in the 1960s. Read had, until that point, been an enthusiast for modern art, as an expression of the contemporary soul in all its agony. George Woodcock explains that he had hoped it would awake humanity to "growing threats to the quality and even the existence of human life, posed by unrestrained technological development", but that Read had plunged into pessimism and "the emergence during the 1960's of something approaching despair as he realizes that the new movements in painting, and particularly Pop Art, are themselves infected by the disintegration from which society as a whole is suffering".[15] The process has continued in the same direction, with the ironic, self-referential and postmodern confirming the failure of our culture as a whole to overcome, confront or even properly question the extent of our social malaise. Everything is about surface, appearance, illusion, novelty, glitter and gleam. We are fed the lies of progress and of "growth", expected to believe that the reassuring images on our television screens reflect a reassuring reality, expected to trust in our rulers, expected to accept all of this at face value and obediently see out our existences in the manner demanded of us.

Meanwhile, of course, millions of people, many of them children, are forced to live in poverty and slavery in order to create the profits that fuel the capitalist system. Countless lives are lost and ruined by wars designed to feather the nests of the same financial vultures, both by securing resources for them to plunder and by providing markets for the murder-machines they sell to the corrupt protection-racket tax-collecting mafia we term "governments". Human misery, tyranny, theft of land and resources, injustice, imperialism, torture are rampant across the world. But none of this seems to permeate beneath the very surface of the mind of the western consumer, for whom the "news" – which may or may not reveal the existence of some of these unpleasant realities, depending on current political expediency – is just a small part of the evening's package of "entertainment" that nicely fills up his or her mind so that it need not be troubled by anything resembling thought.

For many of us, it can be difficult to find one's feet in such a society and make any sense out of one's role. Hermann Hesse's fictional female alter ego Hermine declares in *Steppenwolf*: "Whoever wants to live and enjoy his life today must not be like you and me. Whoever wants music instead of noise, joy instead of pleasure, soul instead of gold, creative work instead of business, passion instead of foolery, finds no home in this trivial world of ours".[16] This is the frustration for those who see behind the flimsy, flashy film set of western civilization and catch a glimpse of the degradation and destruction which it seeks to conceal – how are so many people apparently fooled by this? Perhaps they know really, but just can't face the truth and in order to keep living they have to keep the conscious realisation at bay with whatever mind-numbing drugs come to hand, whether anti-depressants, cannabis, bottles of vodka, internet surfing, shopping, or flickering colourful images beamed into their living rooms.

Is our doomed culture as a whole, as Nietzsche suggests, now "afraid to reflect"?[17] If so, perhaps we have created for ourselves – to prevent that reflection – a culture where the bulk of the population are incapable of understanding the world they live in, are ignorant as to its history and indifferent as to its future. René Guénon detects in the modern world "a change that is the direct opposite of 'progress', amounting indeed to a veritable regression of intelligence"[18] and he concludes elsewhere: "There must have been already a depreciation and a dwindling of intellectuality for material progress to become important enough to overstep certain bounds; but once this movement had started, with the concerns of material progress absorbing little by little all man's faculties, intellectuality went on growing gradually weaker and weaker, until it reached the plight that we see it in today, with perhaps a still worse one in store for it, although that certainly seems difficult".[19] It is worth bearing in mind that "today" for Guénon was 1924 – a still worse fate was indeed waiting for us in the decades to come!

The theme of intellectual regression is taken up again by Marcuse in the 1960s when he complains that the modern cultural language "constantly imposes *images*, militates against the development and expression of *concepts*. In its immediacy and directness, it impedes conceptual thinking; thus, it impedes thinking".[20] Baudrillard condemns the "absence of reflection" in our culture[21] and Jensen, an outspoken twenty-first century critic of industrial civilization, likewise sees lack of thought as a root cause of our malaise: "This culture devalues introspection, and many of us are trained to do whatever we can to fill (and kill) time so we never have to be alone with who and what we have become, and so we never can become who we really are and were meant to be".[22]

The one type of "thinking" which is encouraged in contemporary society, is that which pursues purely practical goals. Karl Jaspers comments on this in *Man in the Modern Age*, writing: "There has arisen an enmity to culture which reduces the value of mental activity to a technical capacity and to the expression of the minimum of crude life. This attitude is correlative to the process of the technicisation of the planet and of the life of the individual, wherein, among all nations, there has been a breach in historical tradition so that everything has been placed upon new foundations. Nothing can continue to exist except that which finds its technical rationale in the new world created by the West, but which, though thus 'western' in its origin, is universally valid in its significance and its effects. Hence human existence has been shaken to its roots".[23]

It is increasingly taken for granted that thought only has relevance if it is linked to material gain. Education is being redefined, by capitalism, as training for a paid job. Learning for the sake of learning is pushed aside to be replaced by the anti-values of "entrepreneurship". Oxymoronic phrases such "the business community" are deployed to create the impression of social benefit and even superior high-minded intent behind the frantic buying and selling of things and the accelerating conversion of the living planet into dead products of no lasting value, and indeed of negative impact. The term "anti-business" is laughably wielded as an insult rather than a term of admiration and those who see through the deceit and falsity of it all and yearn for a reconnection to authenticity are urged to "live in the real world".

Quantity reigns supreme over quality to the extent that the very idea of quality, or value, has almost been replaced in terms of differentiation by the artificial, and mostly misleading, designation of price. Likewise, wealth is equated with virtue, despite all the evidence pointing to an inverse correlation. Craftsmanship of any kind is eradicated by division of labour, with "flexibility" and "multiskilling" the desirable qualities for interchangeable global labour units. Passivity and gullibility are regarded as useful traits, excessive consumption and self-indulgence as social duties, while human dignity is stolen from us as we are relegated to the role of obedient drones in our work and in our leisure. No argument can ever be allowed to triumph over the constant bleating that such-and-such aberration is "good for the economy", as if "the economy" had some claim to exist in any real sense and was ever anything other than an apparatus designed to allow a small and unscrupulous percentage of the population to gather money and power at the expense of the majority and the natural environment.

Baudrillard writes of "a sort of fundamental mutation in the ecology of the human species", which has seen our personalities and lives increasingly shaped not by our fellow people but by objects.[24] He talks of the absurdity of production for its own sake, commenting that for today's upside-down culture "everything that has been produced is sanctified by that very fact. Every produced thing is positive, every measurable thing is positive".[25]

The once-noble discipline of science has also long been caught up in this ever-downward momentum away from truth, beauty and value, having been converted into a mechanism to make money, regardless of the social or environmental costs, which have been considerable in both aspects. The knowledge behind the various technological advances has become so specialised, so cut off from any sort of overview, that it has no ethical anchor. Individual scientists find it possible to work on processes which they must know could be used for malign purposes, wearing psychological blinkers that prevent them from seeing the destruction to which they are contributing and for which they should be bearing a heavy burden of guilt that would prevent them from continuing their efforts a moment longer.

It is not enough to blame them as individuals – although they must accept that responsibility – for we have to understand that they are merely manifestations of a world where meaning is fragmenting, where inter-connections are concealed so they cannot disrupt the descent into multiplicity and collapse. Concealed by what or by whom? If we view society and its course as an organism with its own will and direction, we might say that the interconnections conceal themselves, as part of its ongoing history. But if we also regard a society as a potentially healthy body, in which its members would be naturally inclined to act in its best long-term interests, then we cannot easily ascribe to it such negative attributes. Why would a society evolve in such a way as to cut itself off from its own soul, destroy its own thought-processes? Only if it was sick in some way, only if it was indeed suffering from a form of mental illness that is very real, even though it seems abstract or metaphorical because of the unfamiliarity of applying such terms to a collective entity. So we would do better to say that the normal, healthy, interconnections of a society, the neural pathways that enable it to function as a whole, have been blocked by disease – the disease of modernity.

II

FREEDOM OBSTRUCTED

So here we are, this "cut-off race of man",[1] bitter, bereft, and forever in search of a meaning to it all. We have to learn to survive in the environment in which we find ourselves and thus, as Colin Wilson says, we are "forced to develop hard shells"[2] to cope with the complexities of our deadeningly materialistic modern civilization. But that doesn't entirely silence the inner voice that yearns for a golden age, a Garden of Eden, where being alive was the joyful journey we all feel it was meant to be. We know we have been denied a complete experience that should have been our birthright and we try to identify the source of that theft of all thefts.

The contemporary anarchists of Offensive Libertaire et Sociale complain that "in one fell swoop, capitalism manages to take all the magic out of life, destroy every kind of authenticity, autonomy and creativity, while increasing levels of inequality in the interests of a minority".[3] For Oswald Spengler, the problem is defined as civilization – not just *this* civilization, but *any* civilization, which he describes as the inevitable death-bed destiny of a living culture: "Civilizations are the most external and artificial states of which a species of developed humanity is capable. They are a conclusion, the thing-become succeeding the thing-becoming, death following life, rigidity following expansion, intellectual age and the stone-built, petrifying world-city following mother-earth and the spiritual childhood of Doric and Gothic".[4]

But whatever the precise nature of the entity that is blocking our way to collective vitality, to whatever point in our history we care to trace it back, our first step to remedying the situation must surely be to seek clear understanding of what exactly we have been cut off from. "It is as simple as that: we have lost touch with *things*, lost the physical experience that comes from a direct contact with organic processes of nature... We know it – instinctively we know it and walk like blind animals into a darker age than history has ever known",[5] says Herbert Read and his view is echoed by Derrick Jensen when, in describing the mental illness afflicting our civilization, he points out that "a reasonable definition of insanity is to have lost one's connections to physical reality, to consider one's delusions as being more real than the real world".[6] Likewise, John Zerzan comments: "The more technicized and artificial the world becomes, and as the natural world is evacuated, there's an obvious sense of being alienated from a natural embeddedness".[7]

Yes, there is an obvious alienation from nature, from the physical reality of our world, for those of us who live in the ever-expanding urban concentrations that are disfiguring the surface of the planet and draining from it its goodness and strength. But, it seems, there are others who look elsewhere for the cause of our separation from authenticity, who regard the malaise as spiritual rather than earthly. René Guénon, for instance, considers that we are living in "an age at the opposite pole to primordial spirituality" in which people are "so embedded in material things as to be incapable of conceiving anything beyond them".[8]

He and other traditionalist thinkers, sometimes known as perennialists, ascribe the sorry plight of contemporary humanity to its divorce from "belief and practice transmitted from time immemorial – or rather belief and practice that *should* have been transmitted but was lost to the West during the last half of the second millennium AD".[9] For them, there can be no more foolhardy act that to turn our backs on what Ananda Coomaraswamy describes as "the universal metaphysical tradition that has been the essential foundation of every past culture".[10] Karl Jaspers concurs that to do so "is as if a man were deliberately to saw off the branch upon which he is sitting".[11]

So do we have a conflict here, between these various critics of the modern age, as to what has gone wrong? In searching for our paradise lost (or stolen), are we forced to choose between delving down under our feet for the fecund and grubby earth beneath the pavements and reaching up above our heads to a pure and lofty esotericism? Absolutely not. While the mainstream religions may insist on a dualism that would suggest incompatibility, this separation is part and parcel of the disease of our age, the division which has left us stranded and confused. For indigenous or pagan religions, the unity of the two aspects is essential and beyond question. Spirit is nature, nature is spirit. Although this knowledge could never be central to the world-view of a civilization built on disconnection, its truth ensures it will always live on, even if only in the undercurrents of our thought.

Aldous Huxley draws attention to the way St Bernard's spirituality embraces nature when he cites him as declaring: "What I know of the divine sciences and Holy Scripture, I learnt in woods and fields. I have had no other masters than the beeches and the oaks",[12] and Zerzan speaks from the pantheist heart of modern environmental thinking when he warns: "In the industrialized culture of irreversible depression, isolation, and cynicism, the spirit will die first, the death of the planet an afterthought".[13]

The convergence of the soul and the soil continues as we contemplate the nature of the energy from which we have been separated, which Carl Jung describes as "that mysterious and irresistible power which comes from the feeling of being part of the whole".[14] This power is the life-force itself, the *Tao*, "cosmic pulsation".[15] It is this energy that animates us, that steers us, that vitalises us, that feeds and inspires us. It is us, but it is more than us. It is in us and it is in everything. It is not merely raw energy, like the rays of the sun, but directing energy. It contains within it the shaping of things as well as the propelling of them. It provides us, as individuals, with the freedom to fulfil our destinies as we please, but it is also the source of our destinies, the source of our ability to see our own destinies and the source of our urge to fulfil them. The true basis of our freedom, as human beings, is to know that we are animated by this outflowing of life and to open ourselves up to it, allow its genius to flow through our veins and release the potential with which we were born.

"The life of the psyche is the life of mankind," writes Jung. "Welling up from the depths of the unconscious, its springs gush forth from the root of the whole human race, since the individual is, biologically speaking, only a twig broken off from the mother and transplanted".[16] Again, we see how the idea of nature in full flow, of life unfolding as it is meant to, overlaps with the higher kinds of religious feeling. Leo Tolstoy, for instance, writes of "the universal spirit which gets into all of us though we are all individuals and which gives us all the urge to do all the things which are necessary". He adds: "The same spirit which exists in a tree and pushes it to grow straight and to produce seeds exists in us, urges us to be closer to God and brings us closer to each other".[17]

Ultimately our aim in knowing the spirit and knowing the earth is to know ourselves, to understand who it is that we are meant to be. Idries Shah describes how the Sufi poet Jalaluddin Rumi tells his hearers that they are "ducks, being brought up by hens" and "they have to realize that their destiny is to swim, not to try to be chickens".[18] Being just what we are may seem a simple task, but it is the greatest challenge any of us can face in a civilization where our compliance, our obedience, depends on us *not* knowing who we are and thus looking elsewhere – to material possessions, to social status, to national identity – for our sense of identity and self-worth.

How, without the clarity of knowing who we are, can we ever hope to grasp what it is we should be doing with our lives? Harry R Moody and David Carroll recount the story of Hasidic rabbi Zusia who, at the end of his long life, was moved to say, "In the world to come no one will ask me why I was not Moses. I shall be asked, 'Why were you not Zusia?'."[19] With this sense of being oneself and acting accordingly, necessarily comes a dimension of motivation – one feels impelled to act in a certain way because of the energy flowing through one's individual being which animates the authentic self. June Singer explains William Blake's concept of the power of "desire" caused by freely flowing energy in the unconscious: "This is an inescapable challenge to the creative person to bypass the values of his society in favour of what appears to him to be the demand from within himself. As a man comes to know the power which animates him as an indwelling entity of his own soul – then desire takes on a new meaning: it becomes a 'sacred' charge which must not be denied".[20] Huxley identifies a key concept, or merging of concepts, within the Sanskrit word *dharma*: "The *dharma* of an individual is, first of all, his essential nature, the intrinsic law of his being and development. But *dharma* also signifies the law of righteousness and piety. The implications of this double meaning are clear: a man's duty, how he ought to live, what he ought to believe and what he ought to do about his beliefs – these things are conditioned by his essential nature, his constitution and temperament".[21]

Where, though, does it come from, this "essential nature" with which it is so important for us to be in touch? What is the origin of these ideas about how we should live which seem to swell up inside us and direct our behaviour? Baruch Spinoza proclaims that "man can be called free only in so far as he has the power to exist and act in accordance with the laws of human nature",[22] but what are the laws of human nature and where are they set down? Nietzsche provides some kind of answer with his affirmation that "our ideas, our values, our yeas and nays, our ifs and buts, grow out of us with the necessity with which a tree bears fruit – related and each with an affinity to each, and evidence of one will, one health, one soil, one sun".[23] With the use of the word "necessity", he is leading us to the idea there is a real and essential source in nature for what seem like the abstract and individual processes of a human mind. Goethe explored the ideas of archetypes in living nature, with Spengler commenting that "to the spiritual eye of Goethe the idea of the prime plant was clearly visible in the form of every individual plant that happened to come up, or even that could possibly come up".[24]

Applying this further afield, we can posit a latent potentiality, out of which can spring any number and variety of physical manifestations, whether tree, plant, animal or human; a sort of abstract energy forcefield containing the shape of how things are meant to be. Jensen explains that indigenous peoples believe we are guided by "original instructions" and have a responsibility to live according to them – "original instructions presume we come into this world carrying with us advice on how to live properly, how to fit in, how to do what is right; and even more crucially, we come into this world having been given a personal and social framework for looking for that advice, for finding it in our daily lives, in dreams, in our relationships with others, and in these others' actions".[25] Were there to be a blueprint for the workings of the human mind, we would expect to see patterns emerge, to see ideas surface in individual minds, arising from a phyletic memory shared by the whole species, rather than personal lived experience. And they do. It was, indeed, exposure to that very phenomenon that led Read to become convinced of this supra-individual level of ideas. George Woodcock tells how Read had "an apocalyptic experience" of personally seeing the form of the ancient mandala, the symbol of the self as a psychic unity, appear spontaneously in modern children's artwork. At that point Read realised that there existed "a collective unconscious which is in harmony with nature but out of harmony with the world created by abstract systems and conceptual thought".[26]

Jung, for whom Read became editor and publisher, developed and popularised the concept of "an inborn disposition to produce parallel thought-formations, or rather of identical psychic structures common to all men, which I later called the archetypes of the collective unconscious".[27] Jung writes that beyond the intellect "there is a thinking in primordial images – in symbols which are older than historical man; which have been ingrained in him from earliest times, and, eternally living, outlasting all generations, still make up the groundwork of the human psyche. It is only possible to live the fullest life when we are in harmony with these symbols; wisdom is a return to them".[28] He adds that for him the images are "something like psychic organs, to be treated with the greatest care",[29] and stresses that they are neither allegories nor signs, but images of "contents which for the most part transcend consciousness".[30]

Jung does not regard the unconscious as a repository for the repressed elements of the conscious mind, but rather as a resource on which we can draw, a "potential system of psychic functioning handed down by generations of man".[31] He even goes so far as to imagine the collective unconscious as "a collective human being combining the characteristics of both sexes, transcending youth and age, birth and death, and, from having at his command a human experience of one or two million years, almost immortal... He would have lived countless times over the life of the individual, of the family, tribe and people, and he would possess the living sense of the rhythm of growth, flowering and decay".[32]

The existence of a human archetype, an organic blueprint

from which we can draw inspiration and guidance, would be enormously significant at a time when the sense of existential disorientation and unrootedness, and the despair that this engenders, is so very prevalent. We may admire the adaptability that has enabled humanity to bring about and survive (thus far) massive changes to its environment and social patterns, without being constrained by an inflexible and overpowering phyletic memory, but we should not be so arrogant as to assume that we can enjoy good health as a species by trying to totally remove that memory from our mental make-up. Indeed, as we plunge into days of darkness and impending disaster, there is evidently an urgent need for us to plug ourselves back into the collective unconscious and listen to the lessons that it has preserved for us.

How we might achieve that is less clear. Joseph Campbell says it is possible to break straight through to direct assimilation of archetypal images through the process known to Hindu and Buddhist philosophy as *viveka*,[33] but for most of us this is not immediately possible. Since the collective unconscious is permanently in our heads, since it in fact forms the foundation of everything else that is our heads, it would be impossible for us to completely lose contact with it, no matter how alienating, materialist and desensitising the age in which we are born, and dreams are the obvious means by which the archetypes surface and come to our attention. However, it is not necessarily easy to understand the meaning of the images when we come across them and a full interpretation of them along Jungian lines demands a thorough knowledge of myth.

Herein lies a danger for today's humanity, for whom the tales passed down by our ancestors seem increasingly irrelevant to our lives and have largely been replaced in the popular imagination by more contemporary stories: no new "myth" derived from the inauthentic narrative of modern life can answer our psychological needs in terms of making sense of the "original instructions" we receive from the collective unconscious, in terms of leading us, like the Greek mythological heroine Ariadne, out of the labyrinth of our own highly complex psychologies. Campbell stresses that "the symbols of mythology are not manufactured; they cannot be ordered, invented or permanently suppressed. They are spontaneous productions of the psyche, and each bears within it, undamaged, the germ power of its source",[34] and for John Ruskin they are rooted in, and only make sense in the context of, the organic substance from which we arise: "All guidance to the right sense of the human and variable myths will probably depend on our first getting at the sense of the natural and invariable ones".[35]

Psychologist Murray Stein says that "the practical purpose of looking to mythic images – figures, themes, geographies – is to provide orientation for consciousness",[36] and explains that his own method of analysis "employs myth to reveal archetypal patterns of psychological functioning and to elucidate the meaning of psychological events in the lives of contemporary individuals, on the argument that individual persons today are psychologically rooted in the same collective and archetypal patterns of the psyche as were the ancients and primitive people who personified these patterns in the form of myth".[37]

The tales that we would normally classify as myths are only a part of the broader corpus of material through which certain ancient knowledge can be brought into the current age. Perennialist philosopher Frithjof Schuon discusses the universality of symbolism and the role of sacred art in passing on "not only spiritual states of the mind, but psychological attitudes which are accessible to all men",[38] and one of the few ways in which ancient myth still penetrates into the contemporary human mind is through religion – in spite of the layers of hypocrisy and self-aggrandisement that its various organised institutions have built up around the core of wisdom they still preserve. Jung judges that "experience shows that religions are in no sense conscious constructions but that they arise from the natural life of the unconscious psyche and somehow give adequate expression to it. This explains their universal distribution and their enormous influence on humanity throughout history, which would be incomprehensible if religious symbols were not at the very least truths of man's psychological nature".[39]

Whereas myths play a passive role in human life – they are to be listened to and taken in – religions can perform a more active function in encouraging people to act out psychological needs. It is easy, when we look at the pomp and glory of a conventional contemporary religious ceremony, to be repulsed by the sight of such an obviously empty ritual, seemingly carried out for no other purpose than the self-celebration of those taking part and the instilling of awe, respect, fear or obedience in the hearts of the faithful flock whose unquestioning dedication maintains the power of the institution. But originally – before religion was, like everything else, rendered lifeless by the cursed Midas touch of a civilization that values material over spiritual gold – there was a very real purpose behind these ceremonies.

Jung, writing about rites of renewal, explains: "The rites are attempts to abolish the separation between the conscious mind and the unconscious, the real source of life, and to bring about a reunion of the individual with the native soil of his inherited, instinctive make-up. Had these rites of renewal not yielded definite results they would not only have died out in prehistoric times but would never have arisen in the first place".[40] He and Campbell both draw attention to the corollary of the beneficial effects of such rites – the spiritual confusion of individuals and societies that have abandoned such techniques. Jung suggests the result is "nothing less than neurotic decay, embitterment, atrophy and sterility"[41] while Campbell says it may well be that "the very high incidence of neuroticism among ourselves follows from the decline among us of such effective spiritual aid".[42]

In his book *Nature and Madness*, Paul Shepard also points to the loss of rites of passage as a key factor in the mental illness of our civilization, placing this in the broader context of a separation from nature itself. The development of an individual – their ontogeny – is, he argues, meant to be closely linked to the natural world and the stages of life through which we have evolved to pass. He writes: "Among those relict tribal peoples who seem to live at peace with their world, who feel themselves to be guests rather than masters, the ontogeny of the individual has some characteristic features. I conjecture that their ontogeny is more normal than ours (for which I will be seen as sentimental and romantic) and that it may be considered to be a standard from which we have deviated. Theirs is the way of life to which our ontogeny was fitted by natural selection, fostering a calendar of mental growth, cooperation, leadership, and the study of a mysterious and beautiful world where the clues to the meaning of life were embodied in natural things, where everyday life was inextricable from spiritual significance and encounter, and where the members of the group celebrated individual stages and passages as ritual participation in the first creation. This seed of normal ontogeny is present in all of us".[43]

This normal ontogeny would see the mature adult emerge "in a genetic calendar by stages, with time-critical constraints and needs, so that instinct and experience act in concert".[44] Unfortunately, in our own civilization such a natural individual development is rarely possible. Not only have we lost the close connection with the living world which enables a young person to realise their identity as part of a greater, mysterious, whole, but we no longer carry out the rites of passage that enable the transition from one phase of being to the next. The result is that our progression is blocked; we fail to grow up into the adults we were meant to be. Like a plant trying to flourish in a crack in the concrete of some industrial hell-hole, we are stunted, unrealised, a feeble imitation of the proud, vibrant individual we could have become. Discussing Erik Erikson's work in relation to the adolescent's failure to become what he or she could have been, Shepard says: "If the infancy to which they look for an exemplary protocol of growth has been blighted, or if the adult group is not prepared to administer the new and final birth, then the youths create autistic solutions to their own needs and, prolonging the quest of their adolescence, sink finally, cynically, back into their own incompetent immaturity, like exhausted birds going down at sea".[45]

We can find an interesting parallel to this defeated process in the lives of termites, as recorded by Eugène Marais. He describes how the ontogeny of an individual insect completely fails if a crucial stage of its development, a very basic rite of passage, is not acted out when it leaves a nest. "Some of the termites rise high into the air and travel for miles before they settle; others sink to the ground only a stride or two from the old nest. But far or near, fly they must, or the sole object of their existence is frustrated... If those two termites had not flown, none of the events we have watched would have occurred. Instinct is something which only works step by step. If you destroy one step or omit it, then the whole thing collapses. Nature wishes the 'white ant' to spread. If the nests are too close together it would be bad for the communities; therefore they receive wings and must fly. But flight is only one step in their sexual life; if this step is omitted, their sexual life and their existence ends there and then...They *must* crawl out of the nest, they must fly, must settle and lose their wings, then and then only, and then immediately, sexual life begins... The length and distance of the flight is of no importance; it may last hours or only a second; it may cover miles or only an inch. But the force which we call instinct commands – you *must* pass through every stage, you must take every step, or you are doomed".[46]

Like termites, we humans have our "inner calendar"[47] to

guide us through our development and we have, or had, rites, myths and religions to help guide us through the important dates set out for us. When we don't honour those dates, those processes, we fail to become all that nature intended us to be and live out the rest of our lives as lesser, incomplete, human beings, surrounded by millions of others who have met the same fate. We are all trees with no roots, likely to be blown over – collectively as well as individually – by the first strong wind of adversity that blows our way.

The future looks even grimmer, as the cumulative effect of this dislocation inevitably take effect. Parents who have themselves failed to move on from an adolescent psychological state are hardly fit to help their offspring achieve a happy transition to adulthood – indeed, a whole society that is regressed, blocked, insane, cannot realistically be expected to provide a healthy course of ontogeny for its newest generations. RD Laing explains how a human baby born into the modern age is, from the moment of its birth, subjected to forces "mainly concerned with destroying most of its potentialities". He adds: "By the time the new human being is fifteen or so, we are left with a being like ourselves, a half-crazed creature more or less adjusted to a mad world. This is normality in our present age".[48]

We are thus faced not simply with a current problem of alienation from natural stages of psychological development, but an ongoing descent away from collective health, as dysfunctionality is reproduced and magnified through successive generations. As we move away from the natural physical and social environment in which we evolved to flourish, we are also inevitably moving away from our own authenticity and also from the possibility of even knowing what authenticity is, of understanding what we have lost and how we lost it, let alone of rediscovering it. On a more abstract level, we are moving away from truth, from which we are separated by layer upon layer of falsity. The artificiality of the modern world resides not only in the physical trappings of our society, but in our very sense of identity and reality. We have lost touch with the essence of our destined way-of-being to the extent that we can hardly even imagine that such a thing could exist. Instead, we depend on an artificial world of meaning to provide some kind of framework for our existence – but one that is so inadequately superficial that deep down we can never believe in it and are forced to create yet more self-trickery, denial and delusion to enable us to go along with it.

We no longer know our own thoughts and our own selves – even our dreaming is drowned out by the stream of images pumped into our heads by the machine that devours us all. The life-force, the *Tao*, has been blocked by this civilization. "What the mind likes to be is free, and prohibition of this freedom is called obstruction to the nature".[49] With its hard, narrow, shallow, empty creed of dry materialism, modern society denies the magic in life. It corrupts and destroys our religions, wipes out the memory of our myths, prevents us from accessing the innate wisdom which would set us free from its chains, which would feed us the strength to be what we are meant to be.

"There is an order in Nature, and the order of Society should be a reflection of it",[50] says Read. But where nature has been disordered by society, where society in turn suffers from its separation from nature and individuals struggle to find their own natures among all the confusion, we are entering into a deadly spiral of collapse and decay, in which existential authenticity appears a distant and impossible dream. Few would dare gainsay Guénon when he describes an acceleration in the disintegration of our culture and society and warns us that "the course of the development of the present humanity closely resembles the movement of a mobile body running down a slope and going faster as it approaches the bottom".[51]

III

DUMP THE SYSTEM!

The lie of "progress" is one of the most dangerous and destructive ever to have permeated the collective human spirit. The word has been deployed to confuse a particular form of ongoing social behaviour with an abstract quality of merit, of necessity, of improvement and even of destiny. It assumes that there is only one possible future for the human race, and that is to continue our blinkered march towards greater and greater industrialisation, ever-more pathological dependence on technology and increasingly acute separation from reality.

Bound up with "progress" are other words whose meaning has been co-opted and distorted to add weight to a legitimacy that will not tolerate any fundamental challenge. Growth, for instance, no longer simply refers to the acting-out of the natural potential of a child, a plant or an animal, but to an economic system in which endlessly increasing production and consumption of goods is required to feed its own exploitative logic, with the only growth existing in the size of the bank accounts of those who profit from the scam. And to "develop" an area of countryside is to destroy it, to wipe out the whole ecosystem – flora, fauna, watercourses, soil and so on – and replace it with the dead manufactured matter of concrete, Tarmac and brick.

These words, which have ossified into assumptions, have

managed to tie themselves into the very notion of time itself, implying that our moving in this particular linear direction is as inevitable as the passing of the seasons, or centuries, or millennia themselves. Critics are dismissed out of hand with the claim that "you can't turn the clock back" – and yet you obviously can, for a clock, though designed to measure the passage of time, is not time itself and, as an artificial creation of humanity, can be artificially manipulated to record whatever time we want it to. Likewise we can step back from the false connection made between the thing they call "progress" to the actual progression of time, the dawning of new days. The future is not yet written and we do not need to – indeed should never allow ourselves to – accept any particular vision of what it should be. Somebody else's projection of the future, no matter how powerful that person and how loud his or her voice, is still merely a projection and not a reality with which we have no choice but to comply.

Moreover, in order to allow that future to unfold – to develop, to grow! – in its own organic way it is imperative that we dispel this illusion of inevitability in the minds of our fellow humans, that we expose the mind-control mendacity of pre-packaged times to come and reveal the reality of limitless possibilities ahead. Oswald Spengler wholly rejects the notion that a society can continue to move, indefinitely, in one and the same direction: "Each Culture has its own new possibilities of self-expression which arise, ripen, decay and never return".[1] He adds: "I see world-history as a picture of endless formations and transformations, of the marvellous waxing and waning of organic forms. The professional historian, on the contrary, sees it as a sort of tapeworm industriously adding onto itself one epoch after another".[2]

With our own civilization in mind, Spengler warns: "The expansive tendency is a doom, something daemonic and immense, which grips, forces into service, and uses up the late mankind of world-city stage, willy-nilly, aware or unaware".[3]

He judges that behind its "hectic zeal" lies "the despairing self-deception of a soul that may not and cannot rest"[4] and refers to "the metaphysically exhausted soil of the West".[5] Spengler compares the dying phase of a culture with that of an individual: "Finally, weary, reluctant, cold, it loses its desire to be and, as in Imperial Rome, wishes itself out of the overlong daylight and back in the darkness of proto-mysticism, in the womb of the mother, in the grave".[6]

Through his comparisons with previous civilizations, Spengler sets out a cyclical view of history, which Joseph Campbell also explores, albeit on a universal rather than specifically human cultural scale, explaining: "The cosmogonic cycle is to be understood as the passage of universal consciousness from the deep sleep zone of the unmanifest, through dream, to the full day of waking; then back again through dream to the timeless dark".[7] For René Guénon the course of human civilization is a microcosm of this cosmic process and he sees the state of the modern world today as reflecting the Hindu description of a time of materialism and selfishness which comes at the very end of the cycle of great ages: "According to all the indications furnished by the traditional doctrines, we have in fact entered upon the last phase of the *Kali-Yuga*, the darkest period of this 'dark age'..."[8]

As an antidote to the all-pervasive fiction of "progress", the cyclical views outlined by the likes of Spengler and Guénon are welcome, but they do present problems of their own. While they obviously envisage an end to the current state of decay and despair, they also imply a certain inevitability concerning its existence and a certain impotence as regards the possibility of our changing anything. Must we simply accept that we are living out our existences in what Herbert Read terms "this foul industrial epoch"[9] and trust that the great wheel of history will eventually move humanity on to a new age of renewal and spiritual health?

If we look back to, say, the collapse of the Western Roman

Empire, this stoical long-term approach would seem to have its merits – why would anyone living in fifth century Rome waste their precious days worrying about the unhealthy condition of a civilization that was, we now know, in any case close to extinction? Unfortunately, these are very different times. Our civilization is much more malignant in scope and form than any that has ever preceded it and the negative implications of its further continuation are far more serious than anything with which the human race has previously had to contend. Guénon, writing in 1927, warns that "the civilization of the West may not always go on developing in the same direction, but may some day reach a point where it will stop, or even be plunged in its entirety into some cataclysm"[10] and adds: "It is therefore to be expected that discoveries, or rather mechanical and industrial inventions, will go on developing and multiplying more rapidly until the end of the present age; and who knows if, given the dangers of destruction they bear in themselves, they will not be one of the chief agents in the ultimate catastrophe, if things reach a point at which this cannot be averted?"[11]

Many have seen this coming for some time, of course, and the wilfully vague blindness of those who are happy to drift with the flow of "progress" has long been countered by the sharp and urgent perception of those who are not fooled into complacency. Take John Ruskin, who addressed the Mechanics' Institute in Bradford on March 1, 1859, and declared that since "the changes in the state of this country are now so rapid", he had some important questions to put to these advocates and shapers of the industrial age regarding what they had in mind for its future. He asked them: "How much of it do you seriously intend within the next fifty years to be coal-pit, brick-field or quarry? For the sake of distinctness of conclusion, I will suppose your success absolute: that from shore to shore the whole of the island is to be set as thick with chimneys as the masts stand in the docks of Liverpool: that there shall be no meadows in it; no trees; no gardens; only a little corn grown upon the housetops, reaped and threshed by steam: that you do not leave even room for roads, but travel either over the roofs of your mills, on viaducts; or under their floors in tunnels: that, the smoke having rendered the light of the sun unserviceable, you work always by the light of your own gas: that no acre of English ground shall be without its shaft and its engine; and therefore, no spot of English ground left, on which it shall be possible to stand, without a definite and calculable chance of being blown off it, at any moment, into small pieces".[12]

We may no longer see the forms with which industrial capitalism threatens us as being mills, shafts and chimneys, but Ruskin's nightmare has hardly faded – it has, in fact, been surpassed by contemporary reality. Dissenting voices have continued to draw attention to the dangers, to all the damage that we have already inflicted and to that which is even now being planned, and do their best to point out that the technological age is, as Read says, "a disaster that is likely to end in the extermination of humanity".[13] There is this, from Anti-Authoritarians Anonymous: "A time of ever-mounting everyday horrors, of which any newspaper is full, accompanies a spreading environmental apocalypse. Alienation and the more literal contaminants compete for the leading role in the deadly dialectic of life in divided, technology-ridden society. Cancer, unknown before civilization, now seems epidemic in a society increasingly barren and literally malignant".[14] Or this from David Watson in his denunciation of the Megamachine: "Mechanization and industrialization have rapidly transformed the planet, exploding ecosystems and human communities with monoculture, industrial degradation, and mass markets. The world now corresponds more closely to the prophetic warnings of primal peoples than to the hollow advertising claims of the industrial system: the plants disappearing and the animals dying, the soils denuded along with the human spirit, vast oceans poisoned, the very rain turned corrosive and deadly, human communities at war with one another over diminishing spoils – and all poised on the brink of an even greater annihilation at the push of a few buttons within reach of stunted, half-dead head-zeks in fortified bunkers. Civilization's railroad leads not only to ecocide, but to evolutionary suicide".[15]

Kirkpatrick Sale, in *After Eden: The Evolution of Human Domination,* points out that we modern humans, predicted to soon number ten billion, have left not one ecosystem on the surface of the earth free of our influence, transforming more than half the land on the planet for our own use, consuming more than 40 per cent of the total photosynthetic productivity of the sun, using 55 per cent of the world's fresh water, controlling and regulating two-thirds of all the rivers and streams, and consuming a wide variety of plant, animal and mineral resources, often to depletion, at a pace that is estimated not to be sustainable for more than fifty years. He says: "It is this extraordinary dominance by one single biped species that has brought us to the present imperilment of the earth, including the extinction of species, the destruction of ecosystems, the alteration of climate, the pollution of waters and soils, the exhaustion of fisheries, the elimination of forests, the spread of deserts, and the disruption of the atmosphere".[16]

There are difficulties in communicating the extent of our despoliation of nature: attempts to provide the relevant evidence can turn into lists of statistics that others find difficult to read and digest; the continuing degradation can be hard to quantify in precise terms; the alarming pace of the changes means information is out of date almost by the time it has been collated, interpreted and published. Some facts do have a heavy impact on the imagination, though. In their 2009 book *What We Leave Behind,* Derrick Jensen and Aric McBay describe the billions of tons of waste, mainly industrial, produced each year by the USA. They ask their readers to imagine trying to transport it out of the country to dumping grounds abroad in Boeing 747s, which can each carry a load of about 377,000 pounds. This, they explain, would involve 31.5 million 747s a year: "If you're sitting at the end of the runway with your lawn chair and your stopwatch you'd better have a good pair of earplugs. A 747 will be screaming past every 1.3 seconds, twenty-four seven. Picture a nose-to-tail string of 747s launching perpetually. And all of this is just from one country. We haven't even talked about the rest of the industrialized nations".[17]

They note that marine rubbish kills more than a million seabirds and 100,000 mammals and turtles each year, as well as "unimaginable numbers of fish",[18] and that our civilization's output of waste has left "dioxin in every stream".[19] Most haunting of all is the description of an unimaginably vast slick of plastic pollution floating in the Pacific Ocean: "That particular 'Garbage Patch' is nearly the size of Africa. And there are six others. Combined, they cover 40 percent of all the oceans, or 25 percent of the entire planet".[20]

Ultimately, although it is there in plentiful amounts, we surely do not really even need any scientific proof to convince ourselves that industrial capitalism is wrecking the place we live in. How could it *not*? How could it be that all these factories, power stations, processing plants, roads, airports, mines, quarries, oil wells, mills, shafts and chimneys would *not* present a serious threat to the natural world? How could air quality, water freshness or the climate *not* be affected by all that activity? The truism that we cannot have infinite economic "growth" on a finite planet has been in the public realm for so long now that one would have imagined its self-evident veracity, and the implications of this, would by now have sunk into the collective consciousness and brought about some kind of fundamental change of direction.

But no. A critical mass of society still pretends that there is no actual proof there is any real problem, still prefers to believe that things can go on the way that they are for ever, that a shiny sci-fi future is still just round the corner if we keep to the prescribed path of progress. It is happy to regard environmentalists as nothing but cranky killjoys – as if there were any joy involved in slowly choking to death in a puddle of toxic waste on a barren, polluted world in which our daily existence amounts to nothing but an empty attempt to hide away from that unbearable reality by surrounding ourselves with the phoney comforts churned out by the machineries that have stolen from us everything good that we ever had. Richard Heinberg points out that "at present, we human beings – while considering ourselves the most intelligent species on the planet – are engaged in the most unintelligent enterprise imaginable: the destruction of our own natural life-support system",[21] and Jensen reminds us that this is not a reality we can run away from: "There is nowhere, no one, safe from the murderous cult that is this culture".[22]

Spengler, with his cyclical view, still predicts that the endpoint of our own civilization might carry more serious repercussions than those of ancient times, describing the modern development of "a drama of such greatness that the men of a future Culture, with other soul and other passions, will hardly be able to resist the conviction that 'in those days' Nature herself was tottering".[23] Our obligation must be to ensure that there is a future culture that will be able to look back on these times and that, although nature is already tottering as Spengler warned, she remains on her feet and out of the grave which we would inevitably share with her.

The task of raising the alarm, of persuading our fellow humans of the desperate need for action, is unfortunately not always aided by the phrasing of the warnings issued by those who are aware of the menace. Sale, whose analysis of human domination we cited earlier, continues his commentary by saying: "There is some dispute about when the ecological catastrophe as a result of all this is likely to hit us full force, and in what ghastly form, but it is no exaggeration to say that the undeniable scientific and informal consensus is that if western civilization continues its reckless policies and practices toward the earth we are headed toward *ecocide*".[24] Let's consider this closely – "if western civilization continues its reckless policies". If? Policies? He has briefly lost sight here of a reality of which he is undoubtedly aware – the problem is (western) civilization itself. The actions of that civilization are not "policies" that can be altered, but facets of its very essence. Civilization is not some abstracted centre of power that can choose whether or not to carry on in a certain manner – it is that destructive behaviour itself. Civilization is the name we give to the "reckless policies" which cause ecocide and all the time that there is civilization there will be expansion, destruction, extinction, pollution and so on – because otherwise we would not be living in a civilization at all, let alone the western one that has proved so spectacularly lethal.

The problem with Sale's formulation here is that it opens the sluice gates to a whole tide of wishful thinking about the possibilities of reforming industrial society just sufficiently to stave off total ecological meltdown, conveniently leaving everything else just as it is. Maybe if we all stopped flushing the toilet quite so often, or put more plastic cartons in the recycling box, or cut back on the number of holiday flights we took, maybe that would make everything all right again and we could carry on with progress and growth and development without having to worry any more?

This is simply not the case, on a purely physical level. Jensen harbours no illusions about the contemporary Holy Grail of "sustainable development", pointing out: "It is an oxymoron, since 'development' is a euphemism in this case for industrialization, which is by definition unsustainable; in fact, industrialization is utterly, irrevocably, and functionally antithetical to sustainability".[25] And, reminding us of the only way that the planet can be saved from industrial civilization, he says: "To stop a train, you dismantle the infrastructure that allows the train to run. To curtail global warming, you dismantle the infrastructure that causes global warming".[26]

Needless to say, the cyclical vision of history also leaves no room for the woolly-minded suggestion of a civilization-lite that could reform itself from within and become something nice and cuddly. Guénon describes the final phase of the dark age of *Kali-Yuga* as "the state of dissolution from which it is impossible to emerge other than by a cataclysm, since it is not a mere readjustment that is necessary at such a stage, but a complete renovation".[27] Expanding on this, he writes: "The course of the manifested world toward its substantial pole ends at last in a 'reversal', which brings it back, by an instantaneous transmutation, to its essential pole; and it may be added that, in view of this instantaneity, and contrary to certain erroneous conceptions of the cyclical movement, there can be no 'reascent' of an exterior order following the 'descent', the course of manifestation as such being always descending from the beginning to the end".[28]

But regardless of whether or not we regard such models as valid, we must face the fact that even if it were possible to put on hold the most damaging effects of industry, to find some ingenious way of mitigating the destructive impact of our civilization so that it was no longer immediately threatening our existence, the long-term problem would still not have been banished. We would still be left with the mindset that has led to the state of the world today. We would still be looking to a future built on expansion, development, economic growth. We would still be valuing quantity over quality, still be trapped in the need to create artificial needs to stimulate production, still be alienated from our environment and cut off from our collective unconscious, still be unable to access our own authentic identity and fulfil the potential with which we were born.

All we would have done, by reining back the effects of industrialisation with some kind of short-term fix, would have been to have postponed the catastrophe. Since, in fact, it is not possible to slow down the destruction of the ecosystem while continuing our civilization, this is a purely hypothetical argument, but one that points to the truth that we cannot afford to evade the issue and pretend that we have any answers, that we ever could have any answers, to the rather urgent issue of our planet being rendered uninhabitable – apart from the one common-sense response that we have been taught to consider not only deeply undesirable but also impossible. We should not be ashamed, or embarrassed, to shout out loud that we very much want the human race, and the other species with which we share the globe, to survive the current assault and that we are prepared to sacrifice whatever it takes to ensure this happens. Jensen puts it bluntly when he declares that "if we don't stop them from killing the planet, nothing else matters"[29] and another commentator even more so when he concludes: "It would be better to dump the whole stinking system and take the consequences".[30]

IV

THE LIE OF DEMOCRACY

Were the democracy in which we nominally live anything more than a sham, there would hardly be a need to discuss the way in which we could bring about the massive and fundamental change to our society which we have seen to be so necessary. We would put our case to our fellow citizens and, if we persuaded them, the due processes would ensure that the idea became collective policy. But this is not how things really happen!

No sooner had the game of parliamentary elections been devised than people realised it was rigged one, with Pierre-Joseph Proudhon famously declaring that "Universal Suffrage is the Counter-Revolution"[1] and Michael Bakunin later writing: "Men once believed that the establishment of universal suffrage would guarantee the freedom of the people. That, alas, was a great illusion..."[2] Others could see the same thing. René Guénon, for instance, comments in 1927 that "the great ability of those who are in control in the modern world lies in making the people believe that they are governing themselves... It was to create this illusion that 'universal suffrage' was invented: the law is supposed to be made by the opinion of the majority, but what is overlooked is that this opinion is something that can very easily be guided and modified; it is always possible, by means of suitable suggestions, to arouse, as may be desired, currents moving in this or that direction".[3]

Oswald Spengler notes in 1928 that "in actuality the freedom of public opinion involves the preparation of public opinion, which costs money; and the freedom of the press brings with it the question of possession of the press, which again is a matter of money; and with the franchise comes electioneering, in which he who pays the piper calls the tune".[4] He adds: "That a franchise should work even approximately as the idealist supposes it to work presumes the absence of any organized leadership working on the electors (in *its* interest) to the extent that its available money permits. As soon as such leadership does appear, the vote ceases to possess anything more than the significance of an opinion recorded by the multitude on the individual organizations, over whose structure it possesses in the end not the slightest positive influence".[5]

For a neat summary of the reality, we need hardly look further than the anarchist dictum that if voting changed anything they would have banned it by now. The capitalist-industrial world order is not going to deliberately leave open the possibility that it could be dismantled by the population off which it feeds and be forced to watch its wealth and dominion confiscated. That same principle can be seen, like a seam in the rock, through every layer of potential political involvement open to those of us outside the plutocratic core. John F Kennedy once said that "those who make peaceful revolution impossible make violent revolution inevitable",[6] but it goes without saying that the authorities in the capitalist heartlands have now made violent revolution pretty much impossible as well.

All-out military war on restive elements of the population has not so far proved necessary to maintain firm control and so the preferred position of apparent government by consent can be maintained. But occasionally events rattle our rulers to such an extent that the mask slips a little and we catch a glimpse of what lies in store for us if ever levels of resistance were to seriously threaten the status quo. The 2011 riots in England prompted not only threats to deploy the army on the streets (where they have, of course, long been deployed to maintain British control of Northern Ireland), but also a rash of harsh sentencing by the courts that brought to mind the historically arrogant attitude of the elite towards lower-order rebels of centuries past.

There can be little doubt that in the instance of London developing a revolutionary situation in which a large crowd broke through police lines and rushed towards the Houses of Parliament, or Buckingham Palace, to enact popular justice on their oppressors, they would be gunned down mercilessly with all the firepower the heavily-militarised British state could muster. What would happen after that, with the "benign" legitimacy of the state severely undermined, is another matter, of course, and there is certainly no intention here to dissuade dreams of revolution or insurrection on the grounds that they could never succeed. However, the fact remains that the British state, along with others of a similar kind, would stop at nothing to protect its power – as witnessed by its actions up to this point, designed to ensure that dissidents can never push events so far that the state is forced to reveal itself to all as the callous, murderous beast that it has always been.

This is not the place to explore in any detail the cogs, fly-wheels and pistons that make up the machineries of permanent oppression. A central role is, of course, played by the law and all the assumptions it makes, all the distance it manages to put between what we all know is right or wrong and what it defines as legal or illegal. Worse than that is that the state does not even abide by the rules of the game it has devised to protect the interests of those it serves. The uniformed mercenary thugs it uses to physically attack dissenters on the streets can never be found guilty of the offences for which the rest of us are all-too-prone to be prosecuted – even when they have maimed or killed. The state knows no restraint on its self-given right to lie and cheat in order to advance its own agenda and stifle voices of protest. It uses the money it extracts from the population to employ armies of online "trolls" to create an impression of overwhelming consent and on agents to spy on that population, to snoop on and monitor the slightest manifestation of opposition to the destructive activities of its capitalist sponsors – right down to community groups trying to protect their local countryside.[7] Their role is not merely passive, either. As Tom Anderson of Corporate Watch points out, the presence of undercover officers "can help the police to shape and mould the activities of groups that they have infiltrated" and "undermine and disrupt political activity which challenges the system".[8]

These agents are permitted by the state to sexually abuse their targets[9] and to be involved in any kind of illicit behaviour, up to and including murder.[10] State-sponsored terrorist networks are used to discredit genuine rebels or frighten the public into accepting more and more draconian laws.[11] Surveillance is reaching saturation point and privacy swept away in a goldfish-bowl world where the authorities can read every email or text message, listen to every phone call, log every website visit or credit card purchase, track every movement through mobile phones, number plate reading cameras, CCTV face recognition or RFID (radio-frequency identification) chips.

Protest is only regarded as legitimate when it is disempowering and symbolic not of feisty dissatisfaction but of cowed obedience. On-the-spot punishment for dissent is dished out on the streets by the state's loyal servants, whether in the form of the outdoor mass detention termed "kettling", of arrest or of physical assault. The aim either way is humiliation, determent from future activism, the criminalisation of dissent in the minds of those protesting as well as in the minds of those charged with thwarting their altruistic efforts. Withdrawal of labour, even when legally permitted, is still regarded as wrongdoing and elaborate intrigues hatched to ensure that workers cannot freely assert their rights.[12] Political street stalls are persecuted and prosecuted, venues daring to host meetings of the state's opponents hassled and threatened, employers of "troublesome" individuals informed on the sly about their activities. The very existence of the term "domestic extremists" and of police units specifically set up to hinder their activities[13] tells us all we need to know about the reality of democracy in the UK – a reality replicated, of course, elsewhere.

But the defence system of the capitalist state goes much deeper than these pragmatic manifestations. Indeed, Herbert Marcuse suggests that the traditional forms of protest could actually prove counter-constructive – "even dangerous" – in that they draw attention away from more significant levels of control and, by implying that there is some point in trying to influence the authorities in any significant way, "preserve the illusion of popular sovereignty".[14] The presentation of "reality" plays a key role in ensuring that the state's more obviously repressive activities need only be directed at the small – and thus easily dismissed or vilified – segment of the population who have managed to break through the outer ring of its fortifications by refusing to conform to its prescribed understanding of the world.

We can see it at work, for instance, in the concept of "rights". The "right to free speech", although something many of us are prepared to stand up for on a practical level, implies (or can be interpreted as implying) that it is something that has been granted to us, graciously, by the authorities as part of some kind of social contract. It immediately cuts out of the picture any idea that we are free creatures born on this planet with no obligation to ask or receive permission from anyone to express ourselves, that the definition of something as a "right" is instantaneously the theft of its essence as something that just happens naturally anyway – a similar process to the property developers' proud announcement that they will be "providing green space" in the middle of a housing estate that they have just built over the countryside.

At the day-to-day forefront of this highly effective mind-shaping is the media. While it's easy to identify and combat the brash reactionary propaganda pushed out by some right-wing newspapers, the subtlety of the propaganda techniques employed by the likes of the BBC, with its carefully-fashioned façade of objective neutrality, and *The Guardian*, with its ostensibly more radical stance, are much more difficult to expose and challenge, although organisations such as Media Lens perform a crucial function in demonstrating that it is possible to do so.[15]

A key inspiration for this kind of analysis is the propaganda model of media set out by Edward S Herman and Noam Chomsky, who state: "The mass media serve as a system for communicating messages and symbols to the general populace. It is their function to amuse, entertain, and inform, and to inculcate individuals with the values, beliefs and codes of behavior that will integrate them into the institutional structures of the larger society. In a world of concentrated wealth and major conflicts of class interest, to fulfill this role requires systematic propaganda".[16] They explain: "The raw material of news must pass through successive filters, leaving only the cleansed residue fit to print. They fix the premises of discourse and interpretation, and the definition of what is newsworthy in the first place, and they explain the basis and operations of what amount to propaganda campaigns,"[17] and they suggest that the propaganda is so sophisticated, so successful, that the journalists churning it out can still believe they are objective commentators: "Within the limits of the filter constraints they often are objective; the constraints are so powerful, and are built into the system in such a fundamental way, that alternative bases of news choice are hardly imaginable".[18]

One area where the media has difficulty constraining public

opinion is on the environment – hardly surprisingly, since it is so painfully obvious that we are rapidly destroying the living flesh of our planet. In her book *Global Spin: The Corporate Assault on Environmentalism*, Sharon Beder cites evidence that – despite the constant propaganda with which they are bombarded – the majority of people in most countries regard the protection of nature as more important than the permanent capitalist demand for economic growth: "Yet this widespread public concern is not translating into government action because of the activities of large corporations that are seeking to subvert or manipulate the popular will".[19] She describes a corporate subversion of the green movement, using "greenwashing" spin and phoney "astroturf" (rather than grassroots) campaigns, that she regards as being "a response to the effective exercise of democratic power by citizen and environmental activists two decades earlier".[20]

Beder explains: "Corporations clearly have far greater financial resources at their disposal. As pressure groups, they can invest millions of dollars into grassroots organising, polls, lawyers, computer and satellite technology, video news releases, and professional advice to put their case directly to politicians and government officials and to garner public support".[21] She identifies a covert form of power which is one of the goals of this corporate conspiracy – the ability to set the political agenda and shape perceptions: "Corporations seek not only to influence legislation and regulation but also to define the agenda – what it is legitimate for government to consider and what can be discussed in the political arena – thereby rendering those groups who have other agendas ineffective".[22]

Thus the capitalist system does not try to persuade us that our environment is not important, because it knows that such an attempt would not only fail, but would also expose to us the unpalatable reality of its own stance on the issue. Instead, it sets firm limits as to how far we can go in challenging industrialism, in terms of what we believe is not just feasible, but even imaginable. Says Beder: "The aim is not to eliminate debate or prevent controversy, because controversy reinforces the perception of a healthy democracy. What is important is the power to limit the subject, scope and boundaries of the controversy".[23]

The public is lulled into a false sense of security by the impression that there are "green" organisations, including branches of government, who care about the environment and who are doing their best to protect it for us. Completely off the agenda is any challenge to the chimera of progress, the fantasy of sustainable development or the impossibility of infinite economic growth, let alone any inclination to "dump the whole stinking system"! The end result is a perplexing gulf between the public perception of what is wrong – the environmental disaster that is unfolding before its eyes – and the public's willingness to do anything about, or even to feel as if it should be doing anything about it. Jensen observes: "If a foreign power (or space aliens) were to do to us and our landbases what the dominant culture does – do their damnedest to turn the planet into a lifeless pile of carcinogenic wastes, and kill, incarcerate, or immiserate those who do not collaborate – we would each and every one of us – at least those of us with the slightest courage, dignity, or sense of self-preservation – fight them to the death, ours or far preferably theirs. But we don't fight. For the most part we don't even resist. How's it feel to be civilized? How's it feel to be a slave?"[24]

If media manipulation is primarily concerned with narrowing representation of the realities of the present and the possibilities for the future, it also plays its part in our society's concealment of the conclusions we can draw from the past. How can anyone with no sense of the history of our culture, our civilization, have any real idea of where we stand today and where we might be going? Guénon comments: "True history might endanger certain political interests; and it may be wondered if this is not the reason, where education is concerned, why certain methods are officially imposed to the exclusion of all others: consciously or not, they begin by removing everything that might make it possible to see things clearly, and that is how 'public opinion' is formed".[25]

Let's be clear – we're not just talking here about the omission of certain key moments, or movements, from the school or college history syllabuses, though that certainly contributes to the overall picture. It's the whole framing of reality that we are dealing with, the conditioning of our minds to accept, as unquestionable truths, certain premises which are required for us to consent to the system in which we find ourselves living out our existences. Part of this is the process of separating individuals from the reality surrounding them and thus of any responsibility for it, of serving up to millions of people, as television does, what Jean Baudrillard terms a "guilt-free passivity".[26] The fake ahistorical world of the mass media exists in its own bubble, constantly referring back to itself, excluding everything that does not sit comfortably with the numbed-down ersatz reality with which it aims to fill the minds of the supine population. This is the psychological totalitarianism of the consumer-capitalist society.[27] "Anyone who hopes to be free must first be aware of their chains and not just carry on living as if they weren't there,"[28] writes Guillaume Carnino, emphasising the gap that has opened up, over the decades and centuries, between modern human beings' perception of the world they inhabit and the rather less acceptable truth.

Colin Wilson regards the grasping of this disturbing state of affairs as the very essence of existential philosophy: "The poet-philosopher has an intuition that man is so completely sunk in delusion that he can never hope to know himself consistently and act upon the knowledge".[29] It's not only information that is denied us, or buried under a mass of false or irrelevant information, but the very means with which to express notions which form no part of the artificial "reality" which we have been force-fed since birth. Marcuse describes how language has been "closed" and "ritualized" to prevent certain ideas from even being formulated, how it "speaks in constructions which impose upon the recipient the slanted and abridged meaning, the blocked development of content, the acceptance of that which is offered in the form in which it is offered".[30] This process renders us unable either to express certain ideas or even to shape them in our brains: "What is taking place is a sweeping redefinition of thought itself, of its function and content".[31]

We have returned here to the same inability to think that we encountered in Chapter I and Spengler also identifies this core problem: "Formerly a man did not dare to think freely. Now he dares, but cannot; his will to think is only a willingness to think to order, and this is what he feels as *his* liberty".[32] At the heart of the phenomenon seems to lie an arrogance: a belief, as solid as it is misguided, that modern humanity represents some kind of apex of cultural evolution and possesses the key to all understanding. This results in a reduction, a squeezing-down of knowledge to fit within the sadly restricted limits of what our thought is able to embrace – as Guénon observes: "Modern man, instead of attempting to raise himself to truth, seeks to drag truth down to his own level".[33]

Marcuse specifically points the finger of blame for this denuded intellectual landscape at positivism, with its conviction that observation and experimental scientific investigation are the only valid sources of knowledge: "positivism is a struggle against all metaphysics, transcendentalisms, and idealisms as obscurantist and regressive modes of thought. To the degree to which the given reality is scientifically comprehended and transformed, to the degree to which society becomes industrial and technological, positivism finds in the society the medium for the realization (and validation) of its concepts – harmony between theory and practice, truth and facts. Philosophic thought turns into affirmative thought; the philosophic critique criticises *within* the societal framework and stigmatizes non-positive notions as mere speculation, dreams or fantasies".[34]

We have already seen how Baudrillard bemoans contemporary culture's denial of transcendence and perspective on itself,[35] and Karl Jaspers makes a telling link between the type of thought-system offered to the modern citizen and the kind of life she or he is expected to lead. He writes: "Positivism... encourages an unceasing activity of the impulses common to us all: an enthusiasm for the numberless and the vast, for the creations of modern technique, for huge crowds; sensational admiration for the achievements, fortunes, and abilities of outstanding individuals; complication and brutalisation of the erotic; gambling, adventurousness, and even the hazarding of one's life. Lottery tickets are sold by the million; crossword puzzles become the chief occupation of people's leisure. This positive gratification of the mind without personal participation or effort promotes efficiency for the daily round, fatigue and recreation being regularised".[36]

When we consider Guénon's statement that "to be fully at ease in a limited sphere, whatever it may be, one must be blind to the possibility of there being anything beyond",[37] we cannot help but wonder, with him, at the convenient coincidence that the "scientific" outlook promoted by empiricism and positivism just happens to chime in "perfect harmony with the needs of a purely material civilization".[38] The same point is made by Robert Ardrey regarding positivism's offshoot in the realm of psychology, when he notes: "Behaviorism was the perfect psychology for a materialist society... Its dogma of human uniqueness and human omnipotence has spread at epidemic pace to infect, to a considerable or great degree, all the sciences of human understanding and much of lay thought as well".[39] Stanley Aronowitz analyses the way that science closes itself off to criticism from outside its own circles by claiming a monopoly on legitimacy for its own restricted *Weltanschauung*: "Since science has defined its methods as the only way to discover truth, the only acceptable criticisms of science are those conducted within the methodological framework that science has set up for itself. Further, science insists that only those who have been inducted into its community, through means of training and credentials, are qualified to make these criticisms".[40]

As the scientific approach has expanded to dominate the whole realm of modern thought, this process must also be identified as having a much wider impact. It is essentially a self-referential model in which "reality" is represented in a hall of mirrors, each reflecting back and confirming the images reflected by the others. In the same way as mass consumer media create their own world, populated by personalities and themes that they have themselves created, so the wider world of human thinking constructs an inward-looking framework of validity for which its own boundaries are necessarily absolute because it has been constructed on the basis that they are so. The artificial walls enclosing the contemporary human mind seem to confirm each others' validity by containing the mind within a system which allows for no wider reality. The words we have at our disposal have evolved, or been manipulated, to enable us only to describe the contents of the space within the framework in which we are permitted to operate. Any thinking outside the framework cannot therefore exist. Any view that comes from beyond the safe walls of generally-agreed reality must therefore be regarded as something else entirely, an incoherent cry of insanity that can only be feared, pitied or mocked – never listened to or taken seriously.

To remain enclosed by this thought-prison is to severely restrict the futures open to us. The "real world" is defined as the one that exists here and now and therefore the "real world" of the future can only be, according to this blinkered outlook, a continuation of the current one, an extension of its assumptions and limitations. Any possible arrangement of the world beyond that is a fantasy, an idle dream, a delusion and not even fit to be given a moment's consideration by the self-appointed guardians of what constitutes potential reality. Thus has our industrial-capitalist system even stolen from us our hopes for tomorrow, indeed our very ability to conceive of having hopes for tomorrow that are not the ones it has piped directly into our brains.

Its fake democracy; its violence, persecution and corruption; its lies and hypocrisies; its relentless propagandising and mind-manipulation; its denial of history, its restriction of language and thought to its own shallow and self-referential level – all of this is designed to demonstrate, in Marcuse's words, "the 'technical' impossibility of being autonomous, of determining one's own life".[41]

V

ANARCHY IS LIFE

In the face of a society which has made it all but impossible to contemplate any alternative to its superficial and amoral plutocentric materialism, something quite extraordinary is called for. What we need is a collective cry of courageous refusal; a ruthless and relentless rebuttal that slices through the centuries-old layers of accumulated and compounded mendacity; an ebullient and explosive ethos that blasts apart the ill-founded illusion of democracy and consensus; a fearless and flaming surge of authenticity that dares to burn off the conceited contemporary clothing of justice, liberty and equality and thus expose beneath them the wretched naked relic of a humanity reduced to a state of near-fatal despair and disease by the forces of tyranny, violence, exploitation and greed.

Luckily, we already have such a set of ideas, such a movement, in the shape of anarchism. In the blood of each and every anarchist flows the need to question everything, to accept no limits to the freedom of the individual and – therefore, as a logical consequence – the community. The anarchist does not merely stray outside the framework of acceptable thinking as carefully assembled by the prevalent system – she smashes it to pieces and dances on the wreckage. No assumption is left unchallenged, no state of affairs regarded as inevitable, no righteous struggle not considered worth waging, no future seen as unreachable. It is not for nothing that street posters in Paris during the uprisings of 1968 declared: "Be realistic – demand the impossible!". This is the whole energy unleashed by the call-to-arms of anarchy: the perpetual power of possibilities denied but never dead.

The philosophical pillars of our prison-society have been rocked time and time again by the eloquence of these critics – as, for instance, in Leo Tolstoy's unshrinking definition of legislation: "Laws are rules, made by people who govern by means of organized violence, for non-compliance with which the non-complier is subjected to blows, to loss of liberty, or even to being murdered".[1] Alexander Berkman likewise writes: "This lawful violence and the fear of it dominate our whole existence, individual and collective. Authority controls our lives from the cradle to the grave – authority parental, priestly and divine, political, economic, social and moral. But whatever the character of that authority, it is always the same executioner wielding power over you through your fear of punishment in one form or another".[2] In his own sweeping condemnation of laws, Michael Bakunin states: "In a word, we reject all legislation – privileged, licensed, official and legal – and all authority, and influence, even though they may emanate from universal suffrage, for we are convinced that it can turn only to the advantage of a dominant minority of exploiters against the interests of the vast majority in subjection to them. It is in this sense that we are really Anarchists".[3]

There is no more powerful life experience for an anarchist than the realisation that all they have been brought up to believe is false, and Emile Henry – a brilliant young student in Paris in the final decade of the 19th century – was no exception. He recalls: "I had been told that our social institutions were founded on justice and equality; I observed all around me nothing but lies and impostures... I brought with me into the struggle a profound hatred which every day was renewed by the spectacle of this society where everything is base, everything is equivocal, everything is ugly, where everything is an impediment to the outflow of human passions, to the generous impulses of the heart, to the free flight of thought".[4]

From its earliest beginnings, anarchism has rejected the idea that certain privileged people can "own" parts of the surface of the planet to the detriment of others, and has looked forward to a tomorrow where property and its associated evils have been abolished. William Godwin writes in 1793: "The spirit of oppression, the spirit of servility, and the spirit of fraud, these are the immediate growth of the established administration of property. They are alike hostile to intellectual and moral improvement. The other vices of envy, malice and revenge, are their inseparable companions. In a state of society, where men lived in the midst of plenty, and where all shared alike the bounties of nature, these sentiments would inevitably expire. The narrow principle of selfishness would vanish".[5] When Pierre-Joseph Proudhon answers the question "What is property?" with the single word "theft",[6] nineteenth century anarchism is provided with a firm foundation for an uncompromising position, which Gustav Landauer restates with admiral directness on the eve of the First World War: "All ownership of things, all land-ownership is in reality ownership of men. Whoever withholds the earth from others, from the masses, forces these others to work for him. Private ownership is theft and slave-holding".[7]

The convention of working for wages, where the majority of us have to surrender so many of our precious days on Earth to tedious and dehumanising toil, simply to allow us to continue living, is one that anarchists cannot accept as either just or necessary. "The worker's liberty, so much exalted by the economists, jurists, and bourgeois republicans, is only a theoretical freedom, lacking any means for its possible realization, and consequently it is only a fictitious liberty, an utter falsehood," thunders Bakunin. "The truth is that the whole life of the worker is simply a continuous and dismaying succession of terms of serfdom – voluntary from the juridical point of view but compulsory in the economic sense – broken up by momentarily brief interludes of freedom accompanied by starvation; in other words, it is real slavery".[8]

It would need considerably more than one short volume to detail all the areas of contemporary life in which anarchy contests the capitalist *con*-sensus. It stands resolutely opposed to the cynical conversion of natural solidarity into a fake sense of collective identity termed "patriotism" – or, when this is harnessed more directly to control and twist the hearts of the population, "nationalism". It sees right through the way this malevolent force is engineered to enable the people's wealth to be siphoned off into buying stockpiles of hideous weapons supposedly for the defence of this fabricated, phoney "nation" and which, if they don't end up rotting away in a heap somewhere before being replaced and updated in yet another lucrative arms industry contract, end up killing and maiming fellow innocent victims of the global money-system who just happen to live in some other part of its empire. And, forever glorying in the variety of human manifestation, it fiercely refuses to allow people to be pigeon-holed, classified, condemned, allocated or stigmatised on account of their gender, ethnicity, sexual orientation, physical abilities or other individual difference, whether innate or chosen.

Most fundamentally, of course, anarchism is opposed to the existence of a state – the main heresy for which it is pilloried by the establishment. Well might the powers-that-be sweat over this central insight of the anarchist tradition, for once the fantasy has been dispelled that people need the state, rather than the other way round, the house of cards of their overall indoctrination of obedience will quickly tumble. It will not be easy to rid the people of this particularly deeply-embedded fallacy, though, as Errico Malatesta acknowledges when he muses: "A man whose limbs had been bound from birth, but who had nevertheless found out how to hobble about, might attribute to the very bands that bound him his ability to move, while, on the contrary, they would diminish and paralyze the muscular energy of his limbs... Suppose a doctor brought forward a complete theory, with a thousand ably invented illustrations, to persuade the man with bound limbs that, if his limbs were freed, he could not walk, or even live. The man would defend his bands furiously and consider anyone his enemy who tried to tear them off".[9]

Always we see the anarchist mind leaping over the walls with which society would confine it, seeing afresh what others have always taken for granted, looking around itself in puzzlement at the holes humanity has dug for itself and fashioning, from its insights, cerebral rope ladders with which we might save ourselves. Consider, in this respect, the conclusion of a passage by George Woodcock on the way in which modern Western life is run according to the mechanical and mathematical symbols of clock time. He points out that the clock dictates our movements and inhibits our actions, turning time from a process of nature into a commodity that can be bought and sold: "And because, without some means of exact time keeping, industrial capitalism could never have developed and could not continue to exploit the workers, the clock represents an element of mechanical tyranny in the lives of modern men more potent than any individual exploiter or than any other machine... In a sane and free society such an arbitrary domination of man by man-made machines is even more ridiculous than the domination of man by man." He then adds, crucially: "Complete liberty implies freedom from the tyranny of abstractions as well as from the rule of men".[10]

Freedom from the tyranny of abstractions – nowhere is the overarching ambition of anarchist thought more vividly expressed than here! Here is a political ideology that is ready to soar into the realm of philosophy without pausing for breath, taking up the call from Herbert Marcuse and Karl Jaspers for an escape from the unimaginative, functional, narrowness of capitalism-friendly positivism. And forget any notion that this supra-political dimension is something that was added on to the anarchist world-view by intellectuals of the second half of the twentieth century – it has been close to its heart all along. In *Statism and Anarchism*, for example, Bakunin condemns those positivists, Hegelians and "present votaries of the goddess of science" who "narrow down this poor life of ours to such an extent that all they can see in it is only the practical manifestation of their own thought and of their own rather imperfect science".[11] He explains elsewhere: "Government by science and men of science, even if they style themselves positivists, the disciples of Auguste Comte, or even the disciples of the doctrinaire school of German Communism, cannot fail to be impotent, ridiculous, inhuman, cruel, oppressive, exploiting, and pernicious. What I preach then is, up to a certain point, the *revolt of life against science*, or rather against *government by science*... the putting of science in its rightful place so that it would never forsake it again".[12]

Bakunin's "revolt of life" is echoed by Landauer when he declares that "anarchy *is life*; the life that awaits us after we have freed ourselves from the yoke,"[13] and here we see the motivation and meaning behind all the rejection of contemporary society and its stifling norms. For an anarchist, this is not how things are *meant* to be; this is not how we are all *meant* to live. Like Malatesta's bound man, we hobble on towards our deaths believing that this is life as it *has* to be, accepting the slave-masters' reassurances that there is no alternative on offer; that we should be grateful to them for keeping us alive with their soggy slices of factory bread and entertained with their second-hand accounts of second-rate televised humour; that the whips, chains and CCTV cameras are all provided for our own safety; that there is no other road than this one, no finer task than breaking rocks, no possible place out there to which we could escape – that there is simply no such thing as freedom.

For an anarchist, the tender green shoot of each new-born child, the precious potential of each wonderfully unique and beautiful human being, is blocked, crushed, destroyed by the steel toe-capped boots of capitalism. Emma Goldman says that the health of society could be measured by a person's "individuality and the extent to which it is free to have its being, to grow and expand unhindered by invasive and coercive authority",[14] and Landauer writes that "anarchism's lone objective is to end the fight of men against men and to unite humanity so that each individual can unfold his natural potential without obstruction".[15]

This, ultimately, is what anarchists mean by freedom. The freedom to be what we are meant to be, to become what we were born and destined by nature to become, if our ontogeny had not been thwarted and distorted. Left to our own devices, freed from the control of the slave-masters, we individuals would co-operate and combine in the way that we were intended to, in the same way as our fellow creatures, plants, insects, fungi and microbes. This is the basis of Peter Kropotkin's classic argument for a society free of state, the harmonious natural order of which humans – and their relations with each other – form part: "The mutual-aid tendency in man has so remote an origin, and is so deeply interwoven with all the past evolution of the human race, that it has been maintained by mankind up to the present time, notwithstanding all vicissitudes of history".[16] As Bakunin says: "Nature, notwithstanding the inexhaustible wealth and variety of beings of which it is constituted, does not by any means present chaos, but instead a magnificently organized world wherein every part is logically correlated to all the other parts".[17]

Natural laws – these are the basis of the anarchist vision of a proper society and the reason why we reject the man-made variety as imposters and destroyers of all that is good and true and real. Bakunin, that fiery messiah of disobedience, explains how these natural laws are of a kind he has no hesitation in bowing to: "Yes, we are unconditionally the slaves of these laws. But in such slavery there is no humiliation, or rather it is not slavery at all. For slavery presupposes the existence of an external master, a legislator standing above those whom he commands, while those laws are not extrinsic in relation to us: they are inherent in us, they constitute our nature, our whole being, physically, intellectually and morally. And it is only through those laws that we live, breathe, act, think and will. Without them we would be nothing, *we simply would not exist*".[18] Natural laws are the interwoven and infinitely complex limbs of a living community, a vital entity that is the only form of "authority" that anarchists can respect, with the difference between a governmental society and an anarchic society being, as Woodcock says, "the difference between a structure and an organism".[19]

Rejecting the pitiful idea that we come into this world devoid of purpose and principle, helplessly amoral blank sheets of living paper on which the state, in its wisdom, must write down the rules by which it demands we should live, anarchists know that inherent laws have already laid down a sense of justice in our souls. "An integral part of the collective existence, man feels his dignity at the same time in himself and in others, and thus carries in his heart the principle of a morality superior to himself," writes Proudhon. "This principle does not come to him from outside; it is secreted within him, it is immanent. It constitutes his essence, the essence of society itself. It is the true form of the human spirit, a form which takes shape and grows towards perfection only by the relationship that every day gives birth to social life. Justice, in other words, exists in us like love, like notions of beauty, of utility, of truth, like all our powers and faculties".[20]

It is precisely because we already know true justice – in our blood, in our bones, in our guts, in our dreams – that anarchists are so revolted by the sick parody that is served up to us by the bigwigs of the state. Our innate sense of right and wrong is mortally offended and the pressure of a true justice repressed, of a natural authority denied, of inherent laws smothered, builds up in our spirits – individually and *en masse*, consciously and unconsciously – and becomes the force behind the need for revolution. This force becomes a living entity itself – not the passive, patient entity that would animate human societies in times when all was going as it should, but an active, dynamic entity that has formed itself with the one purpose of breaking through the obstruction to life that it finds blocking nature's path. For Landauer, this revolutionary entity becomes a source of cohesion, purpose and love – "a spiritual pool" – for a humanity stranded in a desolate and despotic age: "It is in revolution's fire, in its enthusiasm, its brotherhood, its aggressiveness that the image and the feeling of positive unification awakens; a unification that comes through a connecting quality: love as force".[21]

This raw, spiritual, power of revolutionary enthusiasm can enable anarchy to render real and solid its theoretical rejection of the chains of our fake society, for that enthusiasm, that fire, that aggressiveness, is felt by real people, in real towns and cities who take to real streets with real intent. What other hope for change is there than this physical incarnation of the joyous release of the mighty dammed-up waters of justice, of nature, of life? Marcuse certainly finds his inspiration in the prospect of people simply "refusing to play the game" of physical and mental obedience and looks to an eruption of insurrectionary rage from the most alienated and oppressed to break the shackles: "Underneath the conservative popular base is the substratum of the outcasts and outsiders, the exploited and persecuted of other races and other colors, the unemployed and the unemployable. They exist outside the democratic process; their life is the most immediate and the most real need for ending intolerable conditions and institutions. Thus their opposition is revolutionary even if their consciousness is not.

Their opposition hits the system from without and is therefore not deflected by the system; it is an elementary force which violates the rules of the game and, in doing so, reveals it as a rigged game. When they get together and go out into the streets, without arms, without protection, in order to ask for the most primitive civil rights, they know that they face dogs, stones and bombs, jail, concentration camps, even death. Their force is behind every political demonstration for the victims of law and order. The fact that they start refusing to play the game may be the fact that marks the beginning of the end of a period".[22]

Emile Henry, the young Parisian student dismayed by the "impediment to the outflow of human passions, to the generous impulses of the heart, to the free flight of thought" that he saw around him, was impelled by that same force of revolution to hurl himself at corrupt society and try to spark uprising through propaganda by deed. After killing several policemen with a bomb in the offices of a mining company renowned for strike-breaking, and then targeting the swanky upper class Café Terminus with another *attentat*, he was guillotined at the age of 22 in 1894. At his trial he was unrepentant for the deaths he had caused, comparing them with the countless lives taken and destroyed by the callous state-capitalist system (which at the time had been brutally targeting anarchists) and was defiantly confident that the cause for which he was to die would one day triumph over its powerful foes. Henry told his prosecutors: "You have hanged in Chicago, decapitated in Germany, garotted in Jerez, shot in Barcelona, guillotined in Montbrison and Paris, but what you will never destroy is anarchy. Its roots are too deep. It is born in the heart of a society that is rotting and falling apart. It is a violent reaction against the established order. It represents all the egalitarian and libertarian aspirations that strike out against authority. It is everywhere, which makes it impossible to contain. It will end by killing you".[23]

VI

THE COURAGE TO EXIST

It's easy to be a rebel when all is going well; when everything is fun and empowering; when the camaraderie gives us a glimpse of the future we yearn for; when the cracks are appearing in the old order and we seem to be swimming with the tide of history. But what happens when this wave of euphoria has broken; when our comrades have moved on; when the party is over, the squat evicted and general enthusiasm on the wane? This is when the real anarchists are needed, the anarchists who will *always* be anarchists regardless of whether or not they find themselves buoyed up by the warmth and friendship of others with the same aims. But where do they come from? Who are these people who will emerge from among the children of today to become the liberators of tomorrow? What kind of individual could wrench themselves free from the mental and physical confines of our society and brave all the derision, isolation and persecution to take on a struggle with a sense of necessity that is incomprehensible to most of their fellow citizens?

One certainty is that they will have no choice in the matter and another is that their destiny, and others', will be determined by the choice they have to make. As far as the no-choice side of this seemingly paradoxical pairing goes, Hermann Hesse puts it strongly when he writes that "nothing can come of it when the likes of us get married and play bourgeois. We weren't made for that. We were made to be hermits, scholars or artists, saints in the desert... but not husbands and fathers. When we were children, great pains were taken 'to break our wills', as pious pedagogues called it in those days, and indeed all kind of things were broken in us, but precisely not that will, not that unique quality which has been born with us, not that spark which has made us into outsiders and cranks".[1] The issue here is not whether one can combine parenthood with a meaningful existence, which one obviously can, but that some individuals find as they grow into adulthood that they simply do not fit into society – or, at least, the society into which they have been born. That society will inevitably, under the power of its own internal logic, regard the fault as lying with the "misfit", with no questioning as to what it is about itself which the person is unable to fit in with, but for existentialists such as Colin Wilson, Hesse's "cranks" are individuals with enhanced sensibilities: "The Outsider's problem *is* the problem of freedom... a man becomes an Outsider when he begins to chafe under the recognition that he is not free".[2] Outsiders are not free because they are living in a world in which it is no longer possible to be free, in which they can no longer develop into the people they were meant to be, become part of the communities they were meant to be part of. But although they have the ability to sense this, to stretch out their spiritual limbs and touch the inside of the cage that imprisons them, their insight is met not with gratitude and recognition from their fellows, but with contempt and disbelief, for that cage is built from the mindset of those around them.

This mindset denies any possible reality other than the one we live in and those who possess it (or who are possessed by it?) regard themselves, Guénon points out, as being the standard-bearers of common sense and sanity, the "most finished products and the most 'advanced' representatives" of humanity, whereas they are in fact "only beings in whom certain faculties have become atrophied to the extent of being completely abolished".[3] So a person who does possess "certain faculties" – a sense of authentic individual freedom – faces the nightmare of being trapped in a hollow, hypocritical society based on wealth and conformity which blots out any view of a wider world outside its narrow reality. Unable to be themselves within this purely materialist order, in which money prevails over morality, quantity over quality, production over people, they become dislocated, demoralised, lonely. As John Ruskin writes of his alienation within Victorian industrialist society: "Such as I am, to my own amazement, I stand – so far as I can discern – alone in conviction, in hope and in resolution, in the wilderness of this modern world".[4]

It is at this point that the outsider, washed up in this desolate place through no fault or decision of their own, is faced with the choice element of their life path. They can either succumb to the loneliness and hopelessness in one of many ways – such as insanity (as was Ruskin's eventual fate), medication, self-destroying conformity or actual physical suicide – or they can grab the bull by the horns and choose to be themselves in spite of everything. Wilson explains: "This is what constitutes an Outsider. He is uncomfortable in the world. To begin with he fears that this is only because of his inferiority as a human being... Later he decides that it is the world that is 'out of joint', not himself. Then he ceases merely to hate the world, and begins to condemn it".[5] Wilson compares this process to the traditional path followed by prophets and concludes that they are essentially one and the same: "Born in a civilization, they reject its standards of material well-being and retreat into the desert. When they return it is to preach world rejection: intensity of spirit versus physical security. The Outsider's miseries are the prophet's teething pains. He retreats into his room, like a spider in a dark corner; he lives alone, wishes to avoid people... Gradually, the message emerges. It need not be a positive message; why should it, when the impulse that drives to it is negative – disgust?"[6]

It is not easy, though, to turn the feeling of suffocating oppression by society, with all its expectations and prohibitions, into a positive counter-attack. "Choice" is perhaps not a sufficiently strong word – an inner transformation is what is really called for, a transformation which uses the negative as fuel for the positive. Paul Tillich, in his book *The Courage To Be*, writes: "Anxiety turns us toward courage because the other alternative is despair. Courage resists despair by taking anxiety into itself".[7] An enormous inner fortitude is required to take on this existential transformation, as Jean-Paul Sartre acknowledges: "The first effect of existentialism is that it puts every man in possession of himself as he is, and places the entire responsibility for his existence squarely upon his own shoulders".[8]

Karl Jaspers comments: "Today the mental creator has, it would seem, to live, not merely as a solitary, but as if he were making a fresh beginning, in touch with no one, apart alike from friends and from foes. Nietzsche was the first outstanding figure of whom this terrible loneliness was the dominant characteristic".[9] He adds that the demands which the situation makes upon man "are so exacting that none but a being who should be something more than man would seem capable of complying with them... One who believes that everything is in order and who trusts in the world as it now is, does not even need to be equipped with courage. He complies with the course of events which (so he believes) work for good without his participation. His alleged courage is nothing more than a confidence that man is not slipping down into an abyss. One who truly has courage is one who, inspired by an anxious feeling of the possible, reaches out for the knowledge that he alone who aims at the impossible can attain the possible. Only through experience of the impossibility of achieving fulfilment does man become enabled to perform his allotted task".[10]

As Jaspers' use of the term "allotted task" indicates, this

existential self-realisation does not just have internal implications for the person courageous enough to go through it – it also involves a commitment not to run away from the hostile or indifferent external world, but to turn and confront it. Wilson writes: "Existentialism is the revolt against mere logic and reason. It is a plea for intuition and vision. It is a plea for recognising oneself as being *involved* in the problems of existence as a participant, not just as a spectator".[11] Here, then, we have the nature of the rebel, the anarchist. He or she is an individual unusually sensitive to the unhealthy state of our world and the limits imposed on his own freedom, who has no choice but to feel alienated from society. She or he has then made the conscious existential choice not to bow down to external pressure, but to draw upon all her strength and courage and assert her own essence and desires in the face of overwhelming adversity.

There will always be those, of course, who insist on typifying outsiders as weak or deficient individuals, who are unworthy of playing a role in our great industrial-consumer utopia and therefore thrash out blindly against it. A more sophisticated version of this analysis is repeated by Paul Shepard when he refers to, and apparently endorses, George Steiner's argument that in the case of a rebel, "the need for rebirth is projected upon the world so that it, rather than one's own childish self, is to be destroyed".[12] While there certainly is a correlation between our internal processes and the way we see the outside world (and, as we will see, the personal quest for spiritual rebirth can be regarded as a microcosm of the larger reality), it seems bizarre to dismiss concern with the wider reality as *nothing more than* a projection of inner needs. As we have noted, Shepard's own work shows how our civilization's spiralling separation from nature, and the absence of rites of passage which evolved to guide the ontogeny of young people, have left us psychologically stunted. The "childish self" invoked by Steiner is a product of contemporary society. It would therefore be entirely logical for an individual wanting to react against that "childish self" to react against society, if not for the sake of his or her own self, then in terms of future generations. Yes, in a healthy natural society, you would not expect healthy and natural people to be bearing a grudge against the whole set-up and might reasonably question their psychological motivation. But having established, as Shepard has, that we are in fact living in an unhealthy and unnatural society, we would surely not be surprised to find that healthy and natural people did not fit in and were discontented with their lives. In fact, we could go so far as to *define* "healthy and natural" as the *inability* to conform to that sick society or to go along with assumptions and demands that would only make things worse for people to come.

It is the sense of social "calling" or purpose, that makes the existentialist rebellion much more than the mere flexing of an individualist will. Murray Stein recounts that when Carl Jung had been through a personal spiritual crisis "he emerged with a strong conviction that what he had learned from this experience carried an ethical imperative both to serve the needs of collective consciousness (culture) in his time and also to honor the unconscious daimon that had plagued and haunted him since his early childhood",[13] and Jung himself describes a person's "fate" as being a kind of propelling "daemonic will" that does not necessarily coincide with the will of the conscious ego: "When it is opposed to the ego, it is difficult not to feel a certain 'power' in it, whether divine or infernal. The man who submits to his fate calls it the will of God; the man who puts up a hopeless and exhausting fight is more apt to see the devil in it".[14]

So the aim of this summoning-up of personal willpower is to shoulder responsibility for oneself and one's role in the world – individual self-fulfilment is the *means* by which we can make ourselves fit and capable of carrying out our "allotted task" rather than the sole *purpose* of our inner work. But, according to Jung, the motivation and strength behind this process also *originates* in something beyond the individual ego – it is the power of the collective unconscious acting through the individual and overriding the narrow concerns of the selfish ego. A power that *emerges from* a collective source and is ultimately *deployed for* the collective good is one that is merely channelled by an individual or individuals and this is what is happening in the case of outsiders in the modern world. The power is the "directing energy" we discussed earlier, the source of our destinies to which we must open ourselves up – but in these circumstances, where society does not allow us to live how we should, the specific potential it releases is to challenge, oppose and attempt to destroy the blockages to the *Tao*, to the happiness for which we were born.

Despite the stranglehold of the dominant materialist mindset over the *conscious* workings of society, the collective human *unconscious* is activated, by its own inability to direct society as it should, to try and correct matters and restore natural harmony. Thus individuals find themselves prompted by Jung's "daemonic will" or William Blake's "desire" to challenge aspects of the society in which they live and take on the heavy burden of responsibility for trying to change it in whatever way their personal abilities allow. In a different world, these individuals would have played another role – perhaps a creative, educational, healing or stabilising one – but in the abnormal and dangerously diseased one in which we currently exist, they are destined to take on an oppositional, confrontational role in a bid to put things right.

We could, for instance, see these rebels as the equivalent of antibodies within the bloodstream, created by the body as a whole to seek out and eliminate the antigens threatening its health and, indeed, life. The "original instructions" that indigenous peoples believed directed our destinies have been modified to account for the dire situation in which humanity (and the planet) finds itself, and now point many of us in the direction of the emergency action required. Wilson writes: "Every time a civilisation reaches its moments of crisis, it is capable of creating some higher type of man. Its successful response to the crisis *depends* upon the creation of a higher type of man. Not necessarily the Nietzschean Superman, but some type of man with broader consciousness and a deeper sense of purpose than ever before. Civilisation cannot continue in its present muddling, short-sighted way, producing better and better refrigerators, wider and wider cinema-screens, and steadily draining men of all sense of a life of the spirit. The Outsider is nature's attempt to counterbalance this death of purpose. The challenge is immediate, and demands response from every one of us who is capable of understanding it".[15]

The difficulty for any individual, of course, is knowing how they fit in with all this. Even assuming they manage to overcome all the self-doubt and loneliness and are able to get in touch with the inner need to do something to combat the disease of the society around them, they can still be left in the dark as to what it is that they are exactly supposed to be doing. We return here to the problem of our contemporary separation from the primordial values that have been passed down over the millennia by successive generations of humanity. We have seen how the arrogance of modern society denies all possibility of meaning outside its own pitifully inadequate frame of reference, making it almost impossible for an individual to draw on the wisdom that should be their birthright. The reduction of thought and understanding to a one-dimensional level, and the corruption of religion into institutions devoted to the protection of power, means we can spend much of our adult lives searching for authentic values by which to live. Jaspers judges that because of this, contemporary man "is, in a new sense, dependent upon himself as an individual".[16] He explains: "He must either advance to the frontier where he can glimpse his Transcendence, or else must remain entangled in the disillusionment of a self that is wholly involved in the things of the world. The demands made of him are such as assume him to have the powers of a titan. He must meet these demands, and must see what he is capable of in the way of self-development; for, if he fails to do so, there will remain for him nothing but a life in which he will have the advantages neither of man nor of beast".[17]

The titanic task for outsiders and rebels is thus to forge a sense of value out of their own existential courage, out of the need to be authentic, and to assume responsibility for doing what they can to enable others to live authentic lives in times to come. Through understanding their own personal freedom and the way in which that stems from, and must feed back into, a collective freedom, they begin to piece together the fundaments of what it means to be human. They are guided in this by the blueprint that lies hidden in the human psyche, but, without the help of the cultural heritage designed to provide them with easier access to it, they must inevitably struggle to separate innate value from personal preference or the will of the collective unconscious from a purely egotistic whim.

The kind of deep and lengthy introspection required for this self-discovery is, as we have seen, made very difficult in a frantically noisy and busy society where the mind is constantly distracted by superficiality and ephemeral detail, and where numbed conformity is often the best tactic for survival. But that is what we have to do before we can return – strengthened and guided by the primordial sense of value we have found deep within us – from the desert of contemplation into the realm of civilization and then dare to take on its power with word and deed.

VII

OUR SPIRIT IS UNIVERSAL!

"How do we go on living, when every day our hearts break anew?"[1] asks Derrick Jensen in his 2011 work *Dreams* – and for many of us struggling to make sense of our existence in this soulless and self-destructing society, this is the key psychological question. Where and how can the twenty-first century rebel hope to find his or her inner courage and authenticity? Jensen himself hints at a possible answer when he says that those who see the universe as meaningless, who feel meaninglessly lonely as they rush around and destroy the planet in a meaningless fashion, are missing out on the truth that "a world of meaning surrounds them, a world of meaning that gave birth to them (back when they were alive, back when they were human), a world of meaning waiting to welcome them home".[2]

This is the world of meaning from which we have been cut off by the disease of modernity. Colin Wilson, for his part, regards his Outsider as being essentially in rebellion against *"the lack of spiritual tension* in a materially prosperous civilisation".[3] He declares: "The Outsider only exists because our civilisation has lost its religion".[4] This is not, of course, a call for people to go more frequently to church, synagogue or mosque. The sort of religion Wilson is referring to has been lost within the very organisations that claim to be its custodians.

As John Ruskin observes of nineteenth century Protestant Christianity: "You might sooner get lightning out of incense smoke than true action or passion out of your modern English religion".[5] Instead, when the soullessness of society extends even to the places where we might expect the soul to be discovered, we are forced to make an inner journey. Karl Jaspers, from an existentialist perspective, describes this process as a "philosophic meditation... by which I attain Being and my own self",[6] but it is more commonly known as taking a spiritual path.

This is a universal concept, though particularly well developed in the philosophy of Sufism – the spiritual or esoteric aspect of Islam – as well as in Hinduism and Buddhism, and its basic aim is to enable us to connect with the 'Divine' and thus know our inner selves. It rises above the exoteric level of religion – all the specific creeds and practices – and aspires to heights, and indeed depths, of understanding that are not only unattainable by us in our everyday contemporary existences, but also unimaginable from the severely self-limiting framework within which are today taught to think. Margaret Smith explains that this mysticism "represents a spiritual tendency which is universal, for we find it in all religions worthy of the name and in all true faiths, and it is often the most vital element in such faiths. It represents, too, a craving of the human soul which is eternal, for it has appeared at all periods of the world's history, far back in the religious teachings of India and China, in the civilizations of Greece and Rome, among Buddhists and Jews, as well as among Muslims and Christians... This Unity, the One Reality, is represented under varying aspects by the mystics, as the Ultimate Source, Perfect Goodness, the Eternal Wisdom, Unclouded Light, Beauty Supreme, Divine Love, God".[7]

Not only is this esoteric tradition common to all humanity, but the awareness of this universality forms part of its wisdom and thus intensifies the resonance between those who partake of it, however separated they may appear to be by the superficial apparatus of their respective exoteric religions. Sufi theorist Ibn al 'Arabi is well aware of this when he advises: "Do not attach yourself to any particular creed exclusively, so that you disbelieve in all the rest; otherwise, you will lose much good, nay, you will fail to recognise the real truth of the matter".[8] So is Idries Shah when he says that "Sufism is believed by its followers to be the inner, 'secret' teaching that is concealed within every religion; and because its bases are in every human mind already, Sufic development must inevitably find its expression everywhere".[9]

Shah's mention of "bases" that "are in every human mind already" necessarily reminds us of the "original instructions" of indigenous religion, of the blueprint for ontogeny set out by Shepard, of Bakunin's inherent laws and of Jung's collective unconscious. The assumption is there of an existing pattern within each one of us, which we each set out to access – the quest for the inner self is therefore a quest for the self in its authentic context, as a small part of a vast matrix of spiritual life and not as the isolated, lonely, temporary blip of random consciousness described to us by contemporary positivism. Mystics see our attachment to the egotistical sense of individual separateness as the primary obstacle in our path to this greater understanding: "You are the cloud that veils your own sun. Know the essential reality of your being,"[10] as Ibn 'Arabi puts it.

The discipline of stripping away that impediment is therefore the first task of anyone embarking on the inner spiritual journey, as it opens up the possibility of connection to the greater reality, in whatever terms one sees it. Andrew Harvey says that in both Hinduism and Sufism the responsibility of the Master "is to burn away the ego completely, so that the Divine Presence can be present. The Master takes the lamp and burns away all the oil so there is none left. At that moment the Divine pours in its own oil and lights the lamp itself. The Divine oil is eternal, the wick is eternal, and the flame is eternal".[11] It is crucial to realise that this burning away of the ego is not ultimately a negation of the individual – indeed, it is the individual's own strength that enables this process to happen – but the development and completion of the individual on a higher level.

Hermann Hesse notes in *Steppenwolf* that "the desperate clinging to the self and the desperate clinging to life are the surest way to eternal death, while the power to die, to strip one's self naked, and the eternal surrender of the self bring immortality with them".[12] This "immortality" arises from the individual's discovery that he or she does not really exist – in the limited and lonely definition of existence presented to us by our society. And if separate life is an illusion that we can learn to see through, then personal death, too, is nothing of any worrying significance. Aphraates, a Persian monk writing in the first half of the fourth century, describes the truth behind individual existence thus: "Every man knows that the sun is fixed in the heavens, yet its rays are spread out in the earth and light from it enters by many doors and windows, and wherever the sunshine falls, it is called the sun. And though it fall in many places, it is thus called, but the real sun itself is in Heaven. Also the water of the sea is vast, and when thou takest one cup from it, that is called water. And though thou shouldest divide it into a thousand vessels, yet it is called water by its name".[13]

Reynold A Nicholson confirms that, for Sufis, individual personality does not survive death, although the eternal essence remains: "As the rain-drop absorbed in the ocean is not annihilated but ceases to exist individually, so the disembodied soul becomes indistinguishable from the universal Deity",[14] and Smith also stresses that we are not dealing here with the darkness of annihilation, the elimination of that inner living spark that makes our own death such an empty and chilling prospect, but with a reconvergence of elements that were temporarily divided, a subsisting within the divine "as the drop subsists when it is merged in the ocean, and the spark when it returns to the flame, no longer as a separate entity, but by absorption and transmutation, for the part has returned to become one with the Whole".[15]

The reward for the individual who undergoes this path of self-discovery through ego-shedding could hardly be greater – it is, for Michel Chodkiewicz, "the unveiling of that which is and always will be the Unique Reality",[16] or, as Paul Tillich says, one's affirmation by the "power of being-itself".[17] The Sufi poet Rumi puts it more simply when he declares "when you give up everything, everything is yours"[18] and this formulation evokes the magical magnification of inner strength that can be found on the universal spiritual path. If we can but discover the resolve to leave behind our precious sense of ego and individual life, then we will eventually find ourselves filled with the infinitely more valuable source of courage and purpose that comes from our reconnection to the greater whole. René Guénon says: "Once this point has been reached, there is no longer any danger to fear, for the road always lies open ahead; any domain, no matter what, can be entered into without risk of losing the way or even of staying there overlong, for its exact importance is known in advance; it is no longer possible to be led astray by error in any shape or form, or to take it for truth, or to confuse the contingent with the absolute. To use the language of symbolism, we might say that one has both an infallible compass and an impenetrable suit of armor".[19]

This "assimilation of the ego to a wider personality",[20] as Jung puts it, is positive in more than one way. From the purely personal point of view it provides, as we have seen, a deep sense of eternal belonging that banishes the anxieties of isolated individual existence. Safely removed from the overwhelming dread of death, which we normally have to struggle to suppress from our conscious thoughts, we are at last able to open up to the nature of our existence and truly be ourselves. Harvey urges us: "Watch the flowers: they open totally in their flower-moment. They hold nothing back, and that is our purpose too: to open fully in our human-moment, and by opening totally, to be in the eternal. Anything that opens totally opens into the eternal".[21] This, in turn, reveals to us the responsibility we have, as a part of the whole, to play our role in its well-being. Without the selfishness of individualism to hold us back, without the fear of social disapproval or even of our own personal death to obscure our intentions, we are set free to act for what we know is right.

Here, then, we have an ideal mental preparation for our rebel, our anarchist, who has been faced with the choice of giving in to despair or finding the courage to stand up and be alive. This is the spiritual journey of self-discovery that she or he must take in order to be strong enough to forge meaning from a world hollowed out by the dead hand of civilisation which demands and offers nothing more than one-dimensional conformity. But there is yet another barrier to be overcome before we can marry the will to action to the strength with which to carry it out – for many anarchists, the very idea of religion is repellent and fundamentally contradicts their world-view.

It is hardly surprising that centuries of hierarchy and misogyny should render religion unpalatable for those whose faith is in freedom and equality. Indeed, the very concept of an anthropomorphic God demanding unquestioning obedience from his flock is obviously unacceptable to those whose core beliefs are founded on resistance to external authority. With the slogan "No Gods, No Masters" almost amounting to a kind of global branding for the anarchist movement, there are important differences and antagonisms between it and the world's organised religions, but that does not mean there is any incompatibility with the esoteric core of religion that lies, often unseen, behind the mask of exoteric practice (and we should stress here that the kind of esotericism we are referring to is not that which considers itself fit only for an intellectual elite). Indeed, anarchism shares some interesting, and relatively recent, historical roots with movements and individuals whose aim is to revive understanding of the universal spiritual tradition – a philosophy which reaches back to time immemorial but from which we in the modern West have now been completely cut off – and to promote its values in opposition to the blinkered materialism of capitalism.

In his biography of René Guénon, the most important writer in the twentieth century perennialist tradition, Robin Waterfield comments on the links between spiritual or "occult" movements in nineteenth century France and the revolutionaries of 1848.[22] He goes on to explain that as a young man, Guénon was invested as a "Chevalier Kadosch" in an obscure mystical order called the Chapter and Temple INRI of the Primitive and Original Swedenborgian Rite by Theodore Reuss (1855-1923), an enthusiast for the music of Richard Wagner who had previously joined William Morris's Socialist League and had become "heavily involved" in anarchist circles.[23] Mark Sedgwick, in his exploration of perennialist and traditionalist movements, notes that Guénon's first major mentor was Gérard Encausse (1865-1916), whose Martinist order was "linked not only to feminism but also to most of the other alternative causes of the time: homeopathy, anarchism, animal rights, and of course anything related to alternative spirituality – Masonry, hermetic occultism, Vedanta, Baha'ism, alternative science..."[24]

Another key figure in shaping Guénon's thinking was the Swedish anarchist artist Ivan Aguéli (1869-1917) who came to live in Paris. Along with his lover Marie Huot, described by Sedgwick as "an anarchist, a vegetarian and an animal rights activist",[25] he achieved some kind of notoriety in the French capital and in 1900 shot and wounded a matador in a protest against the proposed introduction of Spanish-style bullfighting to France.[26] Aguéli also lived in Cairo for a while and worked with another anarchist by the name of Enrico Insabato,[27] before, in 1909, he returned to Paris, where, says Sedgwick, "he became known for extravagant behavior. Quick tempered and given to making lengthy speeches on unpopular subjects such as the excellences of anarchism, he frequently wore a turban or Arab dress".[28]

Waterfield describes how Aguéli was "held in gaol for several months for harbouring an anarchist wanted by the police. During his time in prison he studied Hebrew and Arabic besides reading such writers as Fabre d'Olivet, Dionysius the Areopagite, Villiers, L'Isle Adam and, not surprisingly, his compatriot Swedenborg".[29] He says that while Aguéli was in Egypt, he had become a Muslim and Sufi: "Sheikh Abder Rahman Elish El-Kebir, who was Aguéli's *pir*, or spiritual father, was the restorer of the Maliki rite, dominant in West Africa and the Sudan. He was the son of an even more famous spiritual leader of the same name who had been imprisoned by the British in Egypt at the time of the revolt of Arabi Pasha. The particular brand of Sufism that they taught was based on the teachings of one of the greatest of all Muslim Sufis, Ibn Arabi, who was born in Spain in 1165 and studied in Seville".[30] The anarcho-Sufi Aguéli had a direct influence on Guénon, who was "initiated by Aguéli into the Sufi *tariqeh*, by receiving the *barakah* or blessing at his hands".[31] Guénon and Aguéli went on to collaborate on a review called *La Gnose* and "Aguéli, in the issue for January 1911, wrote an important article on the doctrinal identity of Taoism and Islam".[32]

Even more pertinent was the role of Ananda Coomaraswamy (1877-1947), a friend and admirer of Guénon, who translated his work and dedicated to him a chapter of his book *The Bugbear of Literacy*.[33] Coomaraswamy, an important perennialist in his own right, judged that "no living writer in modern Europe is more significant than René Guénon",[34] but was at the same time an anarchist and a keen student of the work of both William Blake and William Morris. Alan Antliff writes: "Drawing on Nietzsche, Coomaraswamy constructed an individualist bridge between an Eastern religious ethos of enlightenment (Hinduism-Buddhism) and a Western ideal of harmonious social organization (anarchism)... The anarchism of Coomaraswamy represents a compelling instance of cross-cultural intermingling in which a European critique of industrial capitalism founded on the arts-and-crafts was turned to anti-colonial ends in a campaign against Eurocentric cultural imperialism and its material corollary, industrial capitalism".[35]

Frithjof Schuon (1907-1998), another of Guénon's disciples, had a longstanding interest in Native American culture. Sedgwick explains that the interest became more serious in 1946, when the perennialist wrote to various followers and admirers from his home in Switzerland asking to be put in touch with a tribal elder. In response, Joseph Epes Brown, an anthropologist at the Indiana University, sent Schuon a copy of John Neihardt's *Black Elk Speaks* (1932), a best-selling first-person account of the life of the Oglala Sioux leader and *wichasha wakan* (holy man) who had taken part in the battles of Little Big Horn and Wounded Knee. After reading this book, Schuon began to discuss Native American spirituality in his correspondence with Guénon, and he also recommended that Brown contact Black Elk; Brown did so, spending a year with him around 1947-48. The results of that year's research were published in 1953, simultaneously in English and French, as *The Sacred Pipe: Black Elk's Account of the Seven Rites of the Oglala Sioux*, and *Les rites secrets des Indiens sioux,* which became a basic source text for the study of North American religion.[36]

Sedgwick adds that Schuon's interest in Native American spirituality continued to grow, and in 1959 he and his wife visited America for the first time, partly "to help save the Native American tradition from modernity" and were adopted into the Sioux, receiving the names of Wicahpi Wiyakpa

(Bright Star) and Wowan Winyan (Artist Woman)".[37] The exploration and celebration of Native American religion fed into the environmental, New Age and anarchist movements in the USA and beyond, with Jensen's eco-philosophy particularly influenced by indigenous American spirituality and the American anarchist Peter Lamborn Wilson (Hakim Bey) seeing a further twenty-first century reconvergence: "As Capital triumphs over the Social as against all spiritualities, spirituality itself finds itself re-aligned with revolution".[38]

There is thus an overlap not only between individuals involved in anarchism and universal spirituality, but also in the ideas they are expressing. This is not totally unexpected – Peter Marshall, in his history of anarchism, *Demanding the Impossible*, traces its roots back to the Taoists of ancient China.[39] Elsewhere Marshall, himself an anarchist, describes the key discovery of "something all pervasive in the universe, some invisible but palpable presence in all beings and things" which can be seen in Eastern religions and the medieval alchemists' belief in an *anima mundi* (world spirit)[40] and writes: "Ultimately, holistic thinking recognizes that all things come from the One and proceed to the One. All is One and One is All. There is unity in diversity throughout the universe; indeed, the greater the diversity, the more overall the harmony. It comes as no surprise that the Greek word kosmos originally meant both the universe and harmony: they are synonymous".[41] Herbert Read also feels himself to be part of a greater whole, though he prefers to use an image from nature, comparing himself to a leaf on a tree: "Deep down in my consciousness is the consciousness of a collective life, a life of which I am part and to which I contribute a minute but unique extension. When I die and fall, the tree remains, nourished to some small degree by my brief manifestations of life. Millions of leaves have preceded me and millions will follow me; the tree itself grows and endures".[42]

Like anarchism, perennialism is a profoundly

internationalist philosophy, appreciating the uniting truth behind different faiths and overcoming religious and cultural divides by rising to a higher level. It is therefore totally irreconcilable with nationalism, despite the efforts of fascists like Julius Evola to fabricate a nationalistic pseudo-traditionalism. As Guénon says: "All nationalism is essentially opposed to the traditional outlook".[43] The perennialist emphasis on knowing oneself, and the necessity of an inner motivation to do so, is also a fundamental aspect of the anarchist outlook. Stephan A Hoeller writes that the Gnostics knew full well that "no one comes to his true selfhood by being what society wants him to be nor by doing what it wants him to do. Family, society, church, trade and profession, political and patriotic allegiances, as well as moral and ethical rules and commandments are, in reality, not in the least conducive to the true spiritual welfare of the human soul. On the contrary, they are more often than not the very shackles which keep us from our true spiritual destiny".[44]

The mysterious workings of natural anarchy are stressed by Carl Jung when he notes that "it is worth man's while to take pains with himself, and he has something in his soul that can grow. It is rewarding to watch patiently the silent happenings in the soul, and the most and the best happens when it is not regulated from outside and from above".[45] The end result of the spiritual path is also far closer to the anarchist conception of an individual's role than may be apparent to those who regard spirituality as merely a means of escapism or evasion of real responsibility. Smith, for instance, in her account of the early Christian mystics, emphasises that "the monastic life was intended, firstly, to bring to perfection the individual soul, but secondly to enable that soul, when brought to perfection, to be of service to its fellow-men, whether by prayer or by active good works".[46]

The Sufis' approach can also be commended for not stopping short at the separation of inner self from ego and the connection with a greater spiritual whole: they do not prescribe detachment from the world, but engagement with it on a higher level. Shah writes that "detachment of intellect is useful only if it enables the practitioner to *do* something as a result. It cannot be an end in itself in any system which is dealing with humanity's self-realization",[47] and Muqaddem 'Abd al-Qadir as-Sufi argues: "Sufism is totally dependent on a life-pattern, a behavioral mode, a total anthropology one might say, for all one's life-transactions from birth up to death must be in approximation to the wisdom-method of the sunna which the Messenger laid down for mankind and which is the Sufi's whole reason for existing. The climax and gift of living this way is the gnosis and spiritual experience that the pseudo-sufis suggest one can gain in some kind of mental vacuum devoid of any existential transformation of action and life-style".[48]

If we are just temporary physical manifestations of a larger and higher entity, as the primal tradition maintains, then we have a very special responsibility to be what we have to be on the material plane. Indeed, we are the only means by which the abstract whole can have a physical existence and interact with the material sphere of reality – we are essentially each a partial incarnation of the whole. As William Blake puts it: "God only Acts & Is, in existing beings or Men".[49]

Sufi commentator 'Abdul-Karim Jili expresses much the same thought: "His attributes are not completed except in us. So we give Him the attributes and He gives us being".[50] Jili sets out a symbiotic relationship between spirit and matter. The Oneness, or Divinity, needs incarnation in the form of a person, "imposing a finiteness upon him for the sake of manifestation thus made possible in him".[51] When Shah writes that "the Sufi is, by virtue of his transmutation, a conscious part of the living reality of all being",[52] the emphasis should fall squarely on the word "conscious". Patrick Harpur sets out this idea from the perspective of the alchemical tradition when he writes: "The *telos* or purpose of the individual soul, its peculiar glory, is to be the means by which the collective Spirit represents and realises itself – actually bodies itself forth – in the world".[53]

So this is the gift that life can give us – to be present in the world, to be conscious of that fact and to have the ability to act in the material world. Without the spiritual understanding of our part in the cosmos, we tend to act purely for the (futile) sake of our own ego, but by undergoing the psychological processes set out for us by the esoteric teachings of the world's religions, we are able to surpass that childish mode of existence and fulfil our true potential as representatives-on-earth of the whole.

Explaining his own theory of *Existenz*, Karl Jaspers insists: "The life of truth in the realm of the spirit does not remove man from his world, but makes him effective for serving his historical present".[54] He adds: "The reality of the world cannot be evaded. Experience of the harshness of the real is the only way by which a man can come to his own self. To play an active part in the world, even though one aims at an impossible, an unattainable goal, is the necessary pre-condition of one's own being".[55]

Any anarchist would surely recognise the process at work here: a rejection of the falsity of the immediate material world and a search for personal authenticity leads to the understanding of a larger context and the need for a commitment to, and to some extent a self-sacrifice for, the common good, whether envisaged on a local or global scale. As instinctive outsiders, we free ourselves from the chains of society's expectations only to find ourselves bearing an enormous burden of care for the well-being of the community. An extreme sense of personal freedom combined with an extreme sense of collective responsibility – this is the powerful creative tension at the heart of the anarchist psyche. Schuon comments that "just as the most holy man is never entirely liberated from action on this earth, since he has a body, so he is never entirely liberated from the distinction between 'good' and 'evil', since this distinction necessarily insinuates itself into every action".[56]

Here we have a three-way overlap between anarchism, perennialism and existentialism and thus Jean-Paul Sartre could be speaking on behalf of any of them when he declares: "Quietism is the attitude of people who say, 'let others do what I cannot do'. The doctrine I am presenting before you is precisely the opposite of this, since it declares that there is no reality except in action. It goes further, indeed, and adds, 'Man is nothing else but what he purposes, he exists only in so far as he realizes himself, he is therefore nothing else but the sum of his actions, nothing else but what his life is'".[57] Colin Wilson takes up this theme in his *Religion and the Rebel*: "The Outsider's way of thinking is called existentialism. But it might as easily be called religion. It is a way of thought which, like the religious way, regards man as *involved* in the universe, not just a spectator and observer, a sort of naturalist looking at the universe through a magnifying-glass and murmuring: 'Mmm. Most interesting'".[58]

Some anarchists have also been more explicit about the connections between their philosophy and certain types of religious thinking, despite the barriers often constructed between the two. When Read says "I am not a revivalist – I have no religion to recommend and none to believe in. I merely affirm, on the evidence of the history of civilizations, that a religion is a necessary element in any organic society",[59] the key phrase is "organic society". This is, as we have seen, the basis of the classical anarchist opposition to the state. External authority is unnecessary and, in fact, harmful because society naturally organises itself according to its own inherent blueprint. Bakunin sets out his vision of this organic entity in *Philosophical Considerations:* "Whatever exists, all the beings which constitute the undefined totality of the Universe, all things existing in the world, whatever their particular nature may be in respect to quality or quantity – the most diverse and the most similar things, great or small, close together or far apart – necessarily and unconsciously exercise upon one another, whether directly or indirectly, perpetual action and reaction. All this boundless multitude of particular actions and reactions, combined in one general movement, produces and constitutes what we call Life, Solidarity, Universal Causality, Nature. Call it, if you find it amusing, God, the Absolute – it really does not matter – provided you do not attribute to the word God a meaning different from the one we have just established: the universal, natural, necessary, and real, but in no way predetermined, preconceived, or foreknown combination of the infinity of particular actions and reactions which all things having real existence incessantly exercise upon one another. This defined, this Universal Solidarity, Nature viewed as an infinite universe, is imposed upon our mind as a rational necessity".[60]

There is an even clearer connection between the esoteric tradition and the anarchism of Gustav Landauer (1870-1919), who was inspired by the pantheist mystic Meister Eckhart, translated his sermons while in prison and wrote about him in his first major philosophical work, *Skepsis und Mystik*, in 1903.[61] The anarchist notion of an organic society is closely related to the idea of Gaia, a living planet, and this is echoed in the ancient Hermetic view that "the universe is composed of a part that is material and a part that is incorporeal; and inasmuch as its body is made with soul in it, the universe is a living creature".[62] Landauer's thinking is very much founded on this idea of the universe as a "living creature" with a collective soul and he writes that "the psyche [*das Seelenhafte*] in the human being is a function or manifestation of the infinite universe".[63]

For those anarchists wary of spiritual terminology, it may seem as if Landauer has stepped across a line and out of the philosophical territory in which they feel comfortable. But in truth the idea of a society, or universe, animated by spirit or soul is a necessary consequence of any belief in an organic society, that bedrock of classical anarchist theory. What sort of organism do we have in mind if it has no soul? A zombie society? A purely mechanical, directionless, one? In what way could we then, as anarchists, argue that the state is not needed to give it a purpose and shape? There is a danger that in backing away from any ideological contamination from religion, and all which that represents, contemporary anarchists are also turning away from the logical conclusion of their own arguments. Yes, as Bakunin says, the universe is a living entity. Yes, as he adds, you could call this 'God' if you were so inclined. Yes, that living entity has a spirit, a blueprint, that gives it shape and yes, that spirit is the force that anarchists believe is the source of the authentic harmony, the world of meaning, in which we are supposed to live and from which we have been cruelly separated by the blight of property, power and so-called progress.

VIII

CLEANSING FIRES OF REVOLUTION

There is one traditional school of thought that specialises in the transmutation of an ordinary human being into somebody strong and focused enough to withstand and take on the malevolence of current times. The ancient philosophy of alchemy is mostly remembered now as a misguided attempt to turn base metals into gold, but it in fact has much in common with both Sufism and Gnosticism – for Carl Jung alchemy was "a religious-philosophical or 'mystical' movement".[1] It takes the individual through the shedding of the superficial ego-self, the absorption into the collective whole and then the existential rebirth as a conscious manifestation of that greater unity, as a temporary representative-on-earth of the life force. The physical experiments carried out by the alchemists were intended as projections, correspondences, with changes being wrought to their own personal psyches. The base metals from which they worked were the flawed, selfish egos with which we all are cursed and the elusive gold was the state of spiritual enlightenment to which they aspired.

Robin Waterfield describes alchemy as a "Sacred Science" whose central objective is summed up in the Latin phrase *solve et coagula:* "First 'chaotic; 'primal' matter has to be dissolved, ie separated, into its constituent elements, and then reassembled (coagulated) into a new arrangement; a process to be repeated until the pattern of perfection is achieved. This process is also understood by Alchemists to be analogous to death and resurrection for the individual, and indicative of the soul's progress through many different states before attaining perfection".[2] This path of separation, purification and rematerialisation in renewed form is often seen as taking the form of descent into, and re-emergence from, some kind of flaming ordeal on the metaphorical alchemist's stove. In his novel *The Angel of the West Window*, Gustav Meyrink includes this warning for those thinking of undertaking this spiritual experience: "Whosoever shall descend into the chasm shall be freed from any other penance and he whose soul is of true gold shall come forth purified the next morning. And many went down into the Chasm but few returned. For the fiery furnace consumes or purifies each according to the nature of his soul".[3] And Jungian psychologist June Singer asks: "Who can expect to walk in fire and yet live, unless he is willing to take a new view of life, an eternal rather than a limited view? And is it not essential before anything novel can be created that the dross of what was before must be burned away?"[4]

In her book *The Way of the Mystics: The Early Christian Mystics and the Rise of the Sufis*, Margaret Smith reveals the perhaps surprising extent to which alchemical themes and terms crop up in early Christian writings, whether it be St Gregory of Nyssa seeing purification in the "true spiritual marriage",[5] St Macarius of Egypt writing of purgation as by fire "which burns up all the dross within the soul... bringing resurrection and immortality",[6] or John of Lycopolis comparing spiritual experience with the process in which "iron is placed in the fire, and the fire passes into it and becomes one substance with it, the iron partakes of the fire, and assumes its likeness and colour, and no longer appears as it formerly did, but takes on the aspect of the fire, because it has become absorbed in the fire and the fire in it, and so they have become one".[7] The influence of alchemy is particularly clear in these words of

Richard of St Victor: "When the soul is plunged in the fire of Divine love, like iron, it first loses its blackness, and then growing to white heat, it becomes like unto the fire itself. And lastly it grows liquid, and losing its nature is transmuted into an utterly different quality of being".[8]

Smith's work traces the flow of ideas from early Christianity into early Islam, particularly the esoteric Sufi tradition, and she notes that Khalid, son of the Caliph Yazid, "studied alchemy under the guidance of a Christian monk".[9] Tosun Bayrak al-Jerrahi tells us that the great Sufi Ibn 'Arabi "was well versed in alchemy"[10] and this influence is also indicated by W.H.T. Gairdner in his description of how Sufis go about escaping certain confines of bodily existence – in which they are "separated by these thick curtains from Allah" – without falling into the trap of seeking detachment from the world and shirking the responsibilities of being alive. He writes: "The whole purpose of Sufism, the Way of the dervish, is to give him an escape from this prison, an apocalypse of the Seventy Thousand Veils, a recovery of the original unity with The One, *while still in this body*. The body is not to be put off; it is to be refined and made spiritual – a help and not a hindrance to the spirit. It is like a metal that has to be refined by fire and transmuted. And the sheikh tells the aspirant that he has the secret of this transmutation. 'We shall throw you into the fire of Spiritual Passion', he says, 'and you will emerge refined'".[11]

At the heart of the alchemical approach is the understanding of correspondences between different levels of existence – also between the outer and inner worlds – and of projection on to certain objects or realms. Jung explains that this projection is often required because of the extreme difficulty in addressing the nature of one's own inner self directly – "people will do anything, no matter how absurd, in order to avoid facing their own souls".[12] He sees the task of alchemy as redeeming the feminine aspect of nature, the *anima mundi*, which is imprisoned in the elements[13] and trying to produce a *corpus subtile*, a transfigured and resurrected body that is at the same time spirit.[14]

Jung says that an individual who is aware of being part of the divine whole has to project that divinity on to something outside him or herself, so as to avoid the inflation of ego which could result from identifying their specific selves with the divine. In Christianity this is projected on to Christ, and in alchemy on to the Philosopher's Stone: "In the Christian projection the *descensus spiritus sancti* stops at the *living body* of the Chosen One, who is at once very man and very God, whereas in alchemy the descent goes right down into the darkness of inanimate matter whose nether regions, according to the Neopythagoreans, are ruled by evil".[15]

Idries Shah identifies the use of a similar projection in the Sufi tradition where the seeker is given a task to complete, not simply for its own sake but as a means for inner transformation: "It may be an alchemical problem, or it may be the effort to reach the conclusion of an enterprise just as unlikely of attainment. For the purposes of his self-development he has to carry that undertaking out with complete faith. In the process of planning and carrying through this effort, he attains his spiritual development".[16] However, this is not to say that the task is of no importance itself, even if it proves impossible to bring it to a successful conclusion. The whole point of correspondences is that there is a two-way connection involved. When George Steiner, via Paul Shepard[17] describes the adolescent desire to change the world as a projection of an inner need, this is the aspect he is missing. The microcosm is not more important than the macrocosm, nor indeed vice-versa. It is the same process we are describing in each realm, happening simultaneously on more than one level and no less real on one than the other.

Thus the improvement of the individual, though central to the alchemical work and spiritual path, does not represent the limit of its ambition, as the Sufis well understand. Shah writes:

"Mankind, according to the Sufis, is infinitely perfectible. The perfection comes about through attunement with the whole of existence. Physical and spiritual life meet, but only where there is a complete balance between them. Systems which teach withdrawal from the world are regarded as unbalanced".[18] He adds that "the regeneration of an essential part of humanity, according to the Sufis, is the goal of mankind. The separation of man from his essence is the cause of his disharmony and unfulfilment. His quest is the purification of the dross and the activation of the gold".[19] A Sufi dictum sets it out neatly: "Man is the microcosm, creation the macrocosm – the unity. All comes from One. By the joining of the power of contemplation all can be attained. This essence must be separated from the body first, then combined with the body. This is the Work. Start with yourself, end with all. Before man, beyond man, transformation".[20]

This transformation can, of course, be interpreted in a religious light, as it is by Orthelius when he writes: "The *spiritus mundi*, that lay upon the waters of old, impregnated them and hatched a seed within them, like a hen upon the egg. It is the virtue that dwells in the inward parts of the earth, and especially in the metals; and it is the task of the art to separate the Archaeus, the *spiritus mundi*, from matter, and to produce a quintessence whose action may be compared with that of Christ upon mankind".[21] Or it can be applied to the level of humanity, as it is by Stephan A Hoeller when he describes the need for the conjunction of the subconscious and the supraconscious: "the new man and woman must be like Abraxas: with head overshadowed by the Logos of wisdom and insight, with swift feet that possess the instinctual force and libidinal resilience of the serpent. These opposites in turn must be joined and welded together by qualities of true and undisguised humanity, a humanity for which no moral, economic or political apologies are required".[22]

Peter Marshall stresses in his study of the alchemists' art

that they "worked for the benefit of the whole: of society, of the planet and of the universe".[23] Here, the relevance of personal spiritual transmutation becomes even clearer for the anarchist, the rebel, the outsider, whose goal is to change society. Not only does the inner process of purification make him or her stronger for the battle ahead, but it is also an acting-out of, a correspondence with, the desired wider transformation. The imagery with which the alchemists, Sufis and other mystics describe that process of change is very much mirrored in the anarchist tradition, which generally rejects the idiocy of trying to reform a fundamentally diseased system and instead looks forward to the cleansing fires of revolution and the new society that will emerge from the ashes.

Gustav Landauer defines anarchism as "a collective name for *transformative ambitions*"[24] and this alchemical tone is echoed by others, whether consciously or not. Michael Bakunin, for his part, writes: "We must first of all purify our atmosphere and transform completely the surroundings in which we live, for they corrupt our instincts and our wills, they constrict our hearts and our intelligences",[25] and Tristan Tzara's 1918 *Dada Manifesto* declares: "We are like a raging wind that rips up the clothes of clouds and prayers, we are preparing the great spectacle of disaster, conflagration and decomposition. Preparing to put an end to mourning, and to replace tears by sirens spreading from one continent to another, clarions of intense joy, bereft of that poisonous sadness. After the carnage we are left with the hope of a purified humanity".[26]

Emma Goldman, too, says anarchist revolution "is the negation of the existing, a violent protest against man's inhumanity to man with all the thousand and one slaveries it involves. It is the destroyer of dominant values upon which a complex system of injustice, oppression, and wrong has been built up by ignorance and brutality. It is the herald of NEW VALUES, ushering in a transformation of the basic relations of man to man, and of man to society... It is the mental and spiritual regenerator".[27] The same kind of language is deployed by Pierre-Joseph Proudhon in *Qu'est-ce que la Propriété:* "Cast off your old selfishness, and plunge into the rising flood of popular equality! There your regenerated soul will acquire new life and vigour; your enervated genius will recover unconquerable energy; and your heart, perhaps already withered, will be rejuvenated! Everything will wear a different look to your illuminated vision; new sentiments will engender new ideas within you; religion, morality, poetry, art, language will appear before you in nobler and fairer forms; and thenceforth, sure of your faith, and thoughtfully enthusiastic, you will hail the dawn of universal regeneration!"[28]

Is it purely coincidence that anarchists draw from the same well of imagery as the great spiritual traditions in their calls for regeneration? Undoubtedly not, for anarchism arose from the very same culture as those traditions and cannot be separated from them by some scientific demarcation dividing "politics" from "religion". If we can state with certainty (as we have) that individuals in the past (and the present) have straddled the traditions of anarchism and spirituality, then we might well conclude that this is the tip of the iceberg and that under the surface the connections are far deeper than we might ever have imagined. Herbert Read refers to the psychological or spiritual role of anarchism when he notes that "none of its critics has considered anarchism as a long-term process of individuation, accomplished by general education and personal discipline"[29.] and anarchism can easily be seen as a correspondence of the individual spiritual path, the will to self-renewal, projected on to society as a whole.

Of course, to identify too strongly with the projection, with anarchy, at the expense of our own self-knowledge is to run the risk of neglecting our own inner development – for instance, it is quite possible to possess simultaneously a very strong altruistic attachment to social change and yet to be hamstrung by unresolved issues surrounding one's fragile ego, not yet psychologically transformed by any internal spiritual effort. If we fail to address this, we become no better than the deluded would-be alchemists pouring their life energies into the attempted creation of gold while not realising that the process must simultaneously be taking part inside their own minds. But at the same time we should not forget that an enormous and empowering spiritual vitality has formed part of anarchy's soul from its very earliest origins – when Andrew Harvey writes of the Sufi poet Rumi being "a lion of passion trying to teach a humanity of depressed sheep how to roar",[30] he could just as well have been describing these anarchist torchbearers.

Listen to Bakunin voicing his vision of the anarchist revolution which continues to inspire today: "There will be a qualitative transformation, a new living, life-giving revelation, a new heaven and a new earth, a young and mighty world in which all our present dissonances will be resolved into a harmonious whole... Let us put our trust in the eternal spirit which destroys and annihilates only because it is the unsearchable and eternally creative source of all life. The urge to destroy is also a creative urge".[31] Or Landauer, striking a tone worthy of the "religion" that he goes on to invoke: "May the revolution bring rebirth. May, since we need nothing so much as new, uncorrupted men rising up out of the unknown darkness and depths, may these renewers, purifiers, saviors not be lacking to our nation. Long live the revolution, and may it grow and rise to new levels in hard, wonderful years. May the nations be imbued with the new, creative spirit out of their task, out of the new conditions, out of the primeval, eternal and unconditional depths, the new spirit that really does create new conditions. May the revolution produce religion, a religion of action, life, love, that makes men happy, redeems them and overcomes impossible situations".[32] Read hits similar heights of spiritual passion and power when he writes: "Faith in the fundamental goodness of man; humility in the presence of natural laws; reason and mutual aid – these are the qualities

96

that can save us. But they must be unified and vitalized by an insurrectionary passion, a flame in which all virtues are tempered and clarified, and brought to their most effective strength".[33]

So can we go further than seeing the anarchist ideal as a correspondence with the spiritual yearning of the individual – is it, in itself, a form of spirituality or even a kind of religion? Read is certainly hinting as much when he writes: "Socialism of the Marxist tradition, that is to say, state socialism, has so completely cut itself off from religious sanctions and has been driven to such pitiful subterfuges in its search for substitutes for religion, that by contrast anarchism, which is not without its mystic strain, is a religion itself. It is possible, that is to say, to conceive a new religion developing out of anarchism. During the Spanish Civil War many observers were struck by the religious intensity of the anarchists. In that country of potential renaissance anarchism has inspired, not only heroes but even saints – a new race of men whose lives are devoted, in sensuous imagination *and in practice*, to the creation of a new type of human society".[34] Admittedly, Spain in the 1930s represents something of an historical peak for the anarchist movement and since then the intensity to which Read refers has probably waned, but the essence of anarchism remains the same and its potential remains unaltered, whatever its current state of ascendancy.

As to whether or not it could amount to a new religion, we must come back here to the important distinction between exoterism and esoterism. The organisations which we today consider "religious" are by and large devoid of the spirituality we have been examining, no more so than in the West where "in the spiritual sphere, the Christian Church has entirely lost the 'inwardness' of its initiatory practices",[35] as Waterfield says. When the rites have become empty, they can offer us no passage. This is hardly a recent phenomenon, with Meister Eckhart warning some 700 years ago that "to seek God by rituals is to get the rituals and lose God in the process",[36] and the end result is that "religion" has become unattractive to the very people for whom it should be indispensable, those who are looking for spiritual depth and the path of inner and outer transformation.

Martin Lings, analysing the appeal of Sufism, says: "A few of the multitudes of atheists and agnostics in the world are what they are for reasons which cannot be considered as altogether inexcusable. Atheism or agnosticism can be the revolt of a virtual mystic against the limits of exotericism; for a man may have in himself, undeveloped, the qualifications for following a spiritual path even in the fullest sense and yet at the same time – and this is more than ever possible in the modern world – he may be ignorant of the existence of religion's mystical dimension. His atheism or agnosticism may be based on the false assumption that religion coincides exactly with the outward and shallow conception of it that many of its so-called 'authorities' exclusively profess. There are souls which are prepared to give either everything or nothing. The inexorable exactingness of Sufism has been known to save those who could be saved by no other means: it has saved them from giving nothing by demanding that they shall give everything".[37]

Reynold A Nicholson, in *The Mystics of Islam*, also confirms this distance between genuine spirituality – which he also finds in the form of Sufism – and the types of "religion" that most of us have encountered and by which we may well have been seriously alienated. He explains that "the Sufis never weary of exposing the futility of a faith which supports itself on intellectual proofs, external authority, self-interest, or self-regard of any kind. The barren dialectic of the theologian; the canting righteousness of the Pharisee rooted in forms and ceremonies; the less crude but equally undisinterested worship of which the motive is desire to gain ever-lasting happiness in the life hereafter; the relatively pure devotion of the mystic who, although he loves God, yes thinks of himself as loving, and whose heart is not wholly emptied of 'otherness' – all these are 'veils' to be removed".[38] René Guénon has his own definition of religion, which he regards as being on a lower plane than the purity of metaphysics, adding that "a purely metaphysical doctrine and a religious doctrine cannot enter into rivalry or conflict, since their domains are clearly different".[39]

Anarchism is not a metaphysical or esoteric doctrine and thus, by Guénon's reckoning, cannot enter into rivalry with the spirituality invoked by him and his fellow perennialists. This keeps open the possibility of anarchism's compatibility with esoteric spirituality, whatever its status in relation to religion. Indeed, there is no reason why anarchism as we now know it could not be regarded as an exoteric aspect of this universal esotericism. As we have seen, it certainly reaches up in a spiritual direction, providing the necessary bridge to esotericism – more so, indeed than contemporary "religions" which deny the very existence of this higher level by falsely claiming that everything of importance is already included in, and contained by, their shallow practices and doctrines. Like the Sufis, the alchemists and other followers of the primal tradition, anarchists seek the transformation of both individual and society, whose destinies they know to be one and the same. By the fires of their revolution, anarchists aspire to turn the dross of our empty and corrupted civilization into the gold of a free and authentic future.

IX

THE ANARCHIST PARADOX

In the superficial, flattened-out society in which we are condemned to live, people are not encouraged to even try to understand unfamiliar ideas and the profoundest ignorance of a subject is seen as no barrier to the most vehemently expressed opinion. Thus, for instance, there is always the wit (or the half-measure of such) ready to mock the very idea of an "anarchist organisation", declaring the whole concept self-contradictory. He or she is not only unaware of the difference between anarchist and hierarchical concepts of organisation and blissfully free of the slightest doubt about the definitions of both words that have been set out by contemporary society, but also aggressively resistant to any idea of challenging these assumptions, or even to accepting that there exists the possibility of so doing.

The prevailing mindset is so fixed in set-in-stone definitions that it cannot even allow itself to see that these definitions are subjective and limiting. Not only can it *see* no alternative reality, but it cannot even grasp that there *could be* another reality to the one it has been conditioned to accept. It is in order to break through the hard cold concrete of this non-thinking view of the world that anarchists have developed a particular way of presenting their ideas and this is by frequent deliberate use of statements that appear to be self-contradictory. Pierre-Joseph Proudhon's equation of property with theft is an obvious example, or the previously-cited 1968 rallying-cry "Be realistic – demand the impossible!" – along with other situationist slogans such as "We demand games with great seriousness" and "It is forbidden to forbid". These devices are essentially riddles that anarchists present to their fellow citizens, designed to make them think twice and wonder how it is that such apparently nonsensical propositions could ever be presented in all seriousness. The contradictions make them difficult to file away under the categories laid out by conventional thinking and so, for those with a modicum of curiosity, further investigation is required. The key to the riddles, of course, lies in some understanding of the anarchist way of thinking and once the enquiring mind discovers that this exists, that this even *can* exist, the way has been cleared for it to grasp the bigger picture to which it was previously blind. "Question everything!" is the root message that is going out – take nothing for granted, accept nothing at face value or on somebody else's say-so.

This attitude stems from the depths of the anarchist philosophy, which is inherently opposed to rigidity and self-limitation: George Woodcock observes that the very idea of a Utopia, always said by mainstream culture to be the ultimate aim of any revolutionary movement, in fact repels most anarchists "because it is a rigid mental construction which, successfully imposed, would prove as stultifying as any existing state to the free development of those subjected to it".[1] Herein lies a fundamental difference between the anarchist and Marxist traditions, with Gustav Landauer lamenting the fact that it was the latter that came to dominate anti-capitalism for many decades: "Instead of Pierre Joseph Proudhon, the man of synthesis, Karl Marx, the man of analysis, was heard and so the dissolution, decay and decline was allowed to continue. Marx, the man of analysis, worked with fixed, rigid concepts imprisoned in their word casings. With these concepts he wanted to express and almost dictate the laws of development. Proudhon, the man of synthesis, taught us that the closed conceptual words are only symbols for incessant movement. He dissolved concepts in streaming continuity. Marx, the man of apparently strict science, was the legislator and dictator of development. He made pronouncements on it; and as he determined it, so it should be once and for all. Events were to behave like a finished, closed, dead reality. Therefore Marxism exists as a doctrine and almost a dogma. Proudhon, who sought to solve no problem with the thing-words, who instead of closed things posited movements, and relations, instead of apparent being, becoming, instead of crude visibility, an invisible fluctuation, who finally – in his most mature writings – transformed the social economy into psychology, while transforming psychology from rigid individual psychology, which makes an isolated thing out of individual man, into social psychology, which conceives of man as a member of an infinite, inseparable and inexpressible stream of becoming".[2]

In contrast to the near-dogma of Marxism, anarchism is light on its feet and playful in its readiness to embrace apparent contradictions and paradoxes. Indeed the very idea of combining opposites seems to appeal to the anarchist psyche. We see this in Woodcock's declaration that: "At the same time as they proclaim their urgent desire to liberate themselves from the dead hand of tradition, anarchists like to believe that their roots run deep into the past, and the paradox is only apparent".[3] There are two levels of paradox-love here: the one that Woodcock is describing, concerning anarchists and tradition, and the one that he is expressing, as an anarchist himself, by formulating his observation in this way. Peter Marshall does much the same thing when he says: "Most anarchists however do not look back to some alleged lost golden age, but forward to a new era of self-conscious freedom. They are therefore both primitivist and progressive, drawing inspiration from a happier way of life in the past and anticipating a new and better one in the future".[4] Michael Bakunin also shows this tendency in *Federalism, Socialism and Anti-Theologism*: "Only by uniting those two faculties, those two apparently contradictory tendencies – abstraction and attentive, scrupulous, and patient analysis of details – can we rise to a true conception of our world (*not merely externally but internally infinite*) and form a somewhat adequate idea of *our universe*, of our terrestrial sphere, or, if you please, of our solar system",[5] and Herbert Read remarks that "it is perfectly possible, even normal, to live a life of contradictions".[6]

On a symbolic level, the anarchist circle-A symbol also plays with an apparent contradiction, representing as it does the combination of order and anarchy. Its intention here is similar to that of the well-known *Taijitu* symbol of Yin-Yang, combining contrasting elements which are in fact complementary and together create overall harmony – "the friendship of contraries, and the blending of things unlike" as the Hermetic writings beautifully put it.[7] We therefore encounter here yet another similarity between anarchism and the universal spirituality explored by the perennialist tradition. They share a love of the sort of thinking that flows as free as the forces of life themselves, with Robin Waterfield explaining that René Guénon's writing does not provide "a rigid, all-embracing system" but rather that "Guénon believed that living by the Tao meant rejecting all notions of systemization".[8] He adds that, for Guénon, "the articulation of meanings as a whole is the outcome of intuition rather than reason; the facts have an inner coherence of their own and are organically linked at the level of imaginative intuition. The fundamental activity of the Divine Wisdom (*Hokmah*) is one of the free creative expression of imagination, of which on earth the counterpart is the play of a child, or the cosmic dance of Shiva, and the outcome of which is not knowledge but joy".[9]

The important thing about anarchism's joyful "contradictions" is that they are not really contradictions at all, once one moves up to a new level of understanding. This is the general truth about polarities – although two qualities may appear to be at opposite ends of a pole, they are also very much connected by that pole and, from a different angle, they can appear to be one and the same thing. Take the anarchist slogan "love and rage", describing two apparently different responses to life in contemporary society and how we might best change it. The strength and meaning of the phrase stems from the fact that they represent the same thing – caring about life and society, being engaged in some way. This is the anarchist position – a connection to, and a sense of responsibility for, the world outside the individual which can be manifested in various ways within the anarchist whole. There is no need for these differing aspects to be resolved in some fashion, no need for the rules regarding an officially sanctioned anarchist state of mind including watered-down versions of both love and rage to be hammered out by an Emotions Sub-Committee – they are allowed to stand as contradictions that nevertheless form part of an overall anarchist harmony.

When they are thus seen as a unity, the opposite polarity to "love and rage", and engagement with the world, is detachment. And yet, to take the process of transcendence a stage further, engagement and detachment are themselves united by being at opposite ends of the pole of being-in-the-world – the very fact of being able to *choose* detachment depends, after all, on a physical presence. The same applies to the pairing of creation and destruction, a common element of anarchist thought. Polar opposites seen from one angle, they are in fact united by the pole of change, which is the opposite of no-change. But change and no-change are in turn united by belonging to the concept of the passing-of-time, which is also an aspect of being-in-the-world – time being the extension of ourselves by which our existence is manifested. So while oppositions do occur all the time, none of them are definitive and depend purely on the angle from which they are seen, or the level at which they are assessed. The problem with contemporary society is that we have lost the ability to understand this and therefore find ourselves boxed in and cut off by the limits we construct around our thinking.

Waterfield identifies one such division when he notes that in the West the spheres of the sacred and profane are "felt to be in opposition, even hostile, to one another",[10] whereas "Hindu thought has never made a separation between philosophy and theology and has retained a unity which the divisive analytical spirit of the West finds hard to accept".[11] It is this separation that makes it difficult for some modern anarchists to accept that their philosophical heritage and identity reaches beyond the political level and into the realms of spirituality. While it must be stressed again that anarchism is not *per se* an esoteric movement, but a revolutionary political one, its modes of thinking are highly compatible with primal spirituality and very much look like the lower slopes of those metaphysical mountains.

Martin Lings describes how a Sufi mystic is conscious of being, like other men, a prisoner in the world of forms, "but unlike them he is also conscious of being free, with a freedom which incomparably outweighs his imprisonment. He may therefore be said to have two centres of consciousness, one human and one Divine, and he may speak now from one and now from the other, which accounts for certain apparent contradictions".[12] Anarchists relish what Carl Jung refers to as "the difficult operation of thinking in paradoxes – a feat possible only to the superior intellect"[13] and, as they continue their *lutta,* they find, like Karl Jaspers, that "at all times the task is marked by this *contradiction*: independence is to be found in aloofness from the world, in renunciation and solitude – or in the world itself, through the world, participating in the world, but without succumbing to it".[14]

Anarchists know, deep down, that the truth lies beyond their individual selves – in the spirit of anarchy, in the soul of humanity – but that it is only by delving into their own psyches that they will find it. "It is the divine *nous* which has entered into the man that tells him what he needs to know; and with that divine *nous* the man's true or highest self is identical or consubstantial. 'Think things out for yourself', says a Hermetist, 'and you will not go astray".[15] Anarchists know that as well as following the sunlit path of reason, of waking knowledge, they must also listen to the moonlit dreaming of the heart – and that these two apparent opposites are, as ever, the same thing. "The moon transmits indirectly the light of the sun to the darkness of night; and analogously the Heart transmits the light of the Spirit to the darkness of the soul. But it is the moonlight that is indirect; the moon itself, when it shines in the night sky, is looking directly at the sun and is itself not in night but in daylight. This symbolism reveals the transcendence of the Heart and explains what is meant when it is said that the Heart is the faculty of direct spiritual (or intellectual) vision".[16]

This puts anarchist thought in direct conflict with Western thinking, with the mindset of our civilization, which has, as Waterfield observes, "followed for many centuries the path of division, that is of quantification, to the almost total exclusion of the concept of unity with distinctions within it".[17] It also places anarchism in opposition to the religious orthodoxy of monotheism (which is ultimately a dualistic notion of a God outside of his own creation) and in line with the holistic vision of pantheism, or mysticism, in which the Divine is immanent in everything and everyone. As Margaret Smith writes: "Religion normally draws a clear distinction between the Divine and the human, and emphasises the separation between the two; Mysticism goes beyond religion, and while still making a distinction, refuses to recognise the separation".[18]

And yet even here, we instinctively back away, wary of falling into any categorising that will restrict the possibilities of our understanding. Taoists say that no term can be applied to the *Tao* because all terms are specific, and the specific, if applied to the *Tao*, will impose a limitation on the range of its function.[19] If we are to exclude nothing from the encompassing of our vision, we must continue to take nothing for granted, must keep up the anarchist mission of questioning everything. Perhaps the harmony between opposites, the creative tension of the cosmos, comes from a constant state of oscillation, as the Sufis suggest: "For the world's existence is the instant of its nonexistence. Thus the Manifest imposes manifestation upon the first hiddenness, and the world is produced. Next the Hidden imposes hiddenness upon the first manifestation, and the world vanishes. Then the authority returns to the Manifest – and so forth, ad infinitum".[20]

This uncertainty as to the state of matter, including the stuff that makes up our own bodies, is echoed in the discoveries of quantum physics regarding the apparently contradictory wave/particle behaviour of light, leading Marion Woodman and Elinor Dickson to conclude that "that these seemingly irreconcilable modes of behavior, once considered a contradiction to be resolved, are not mutually exclusive and therefore do not demand resolution".[21] In any case, Jaspers says, nowhere will we find the whole, full, pure truth "because it cannot exist in any sentence of human speech or in any living human figure. In our limited view of things, we are always losing sight of the other pole. We touch upon the truth only when, in clear consciousness of the polarities, we approach it through them".[22]

By embracing paradoxes rather than trying to resolve them, by always remaining open to new understanding, new insight and new inspiration, anarchists refuse to demand anything less than the impossible, refuse to aim for anywhere short of the ever-receding horizon, refuse to focus on anything other than an infinity on which we will never be able to focus. Waterfield says that Guénon's work is impregnated with the basic contradiction that everything stems from the Principial Unity or Ultimate Reality "which whilst being the final reference point of all that is said, is yet a reality beyond the grasp of reason or discursive thought".[23] In our roles as human beings, we find ourselves physically present in a world that Jaspers describes as "the meeting point of that which is eternal and that which manifests itself in time",[24] and our sense of orientation lies in both understanding and accepting the implications of this reality.

The poles of false opposites which seem to divide reality also mark it out like an abstract three-dimensional, or four-dimensional, grid. By being mentally able to transcend these poles of our existence, to take on the concept of distinction without division, and work ourselves up towards an ultimate level of metaphysical reality that is beyond our means to fully comprehend, we can at least grasp that the truth is ungraspable. Through our inner spiritual awareness – of which the anarchistic embracing of paradox forms an important part – we can aim to reach what Muslims call the third state of being, the *haqqul-yaqin,* which is "the highest possible experience available to men, that of consciously willed complete realization in all modalities, physical, psychical and spiritual, of the Universal Man united to the source of illumination in a complete identification in which the Source and its recipient cease to be separate. This extremely 'high' doctrine of man has ceased to be treated as a practical possibility in the West... And yet the purpose of all initiation is the attainment of the realization in his or her being of the total possibilities of the Universal Man embracing all mankind in its possibility of perfection".[25]

X

THE POETRY OF REVOLT

The joyful and spiritual dimension of anarchism is not an optional extra, not something that can be discarded – by either the anarchist individual or collectivity – without debilitating consequences. While the circumstances of life under capitalism may grind us down and threaten to reduce our existences to flatness and bitter resentment, anarchism is a source of inspiration that can lift us free from that deadness.

Although we may be treated as if we were nothing but slaves and drudges for the monster of Mammon, we must never lose sight of the fact that this is their lie and not our inner reality. Max Cafard argues that those anarchists "who allow themselves to be defined by the conditions of their oppression" are spiritually poisoned and have cut themselves off from the potential which is slumbering within themselves: "The spirit of the child has been entirely extinguished in them. Their creativity, spontaneity, playfulness and vitality are destroyed".[1] This toxicity risks causing a general paralysis – or at least a severe numbing – of anarchism as a living force, where it ends up abandoning the depths of its own all-embracing vision in favour of a much-reduced social analysis. Frithjof Schuon's warning that religions such as Christianity, when they lose their "transcendent dimension", also lose "a life-giving sap"[2] could equally well apply to anarchism if it neglects its connection to the primal esoteric heights and sinks into the uninspiring swamp of narrowly political theory.

This danger facing anarchism can be identified with the restricting ideological influence of positivism, the philosophy of materialist capitalism which also holds sway over the thinking of much of what is termed "the left". Herbert Read is pointing to this when he writes in *The Philosophy of Anarchism* of the need for a spiritual dimension to life: "It will be said that I am appealing to mystical entities, to idealistic notions which all good materialists reject. I do not deny it. What I do deny is that you can build any enduring society without some such mystical ethos. Such a statement will shock the Marxian socialist who, in spite of Marx's warnings, is usually a naïve materialist. Marx's theory – as I think he himself would have been the first to admit – was not a universal theory. It did not deal with all the facts of life – or dealt with some of them only in a very superficial way".[3] This is something of a theme in Read's writing – elsewhere he comments enthusiastically on George Sorel's *Reflections on Violence* which, he feels, supplies to socialism "the imaginative quality that I found lacking in Marx".[4]

Anarchism is not a closed system based on one-dimensional economic analysis, but an opening-up of the human mind to all the possibilities life has to offer. With its love of paradox and transcendence, its thought patterns evoke not so much the politics of pragmatism as the pleasures of poetry. Read is notably joined in this emphasis by Gustav Landauer, who declares: "We are poets; and we want to eliminate the scientific swindlers, the Marxists, cold, hollow, spiritless, so that poetic vision, artistically concentrated creativity, enthusiasm, and prophecy will find their place to act, work and build from now on; in life, with human bodies, for the harmonious life, work and solidarity of groups, communities and nations".[5] Russell Berman and Tim Luke explain that for Landauer the mechanical approach of pure rationalism results in the dehumanisation and systematic misunderstanding of the interior, subjective world: "The growth of humanity depends, therefore, not on the progress of science but rather on the metaphorical mediations of art which can lead to a regeneration of social spirituality, of *Geist*".[6]

The figure of the poet, or artist of any kind, is also similar in many respects to that of the anarchist. He or she is often an outsider of some kind – in current society this is almost inevitable as the poetic and artistic spirit is pitched against the intrinsically antithetical non-values of commercialism – and thence becomes a rebel. The first feeling to be expressed will therefore often be an angry reaction to the world into which the poet has, through no choice of their own, emerged. Read, who says that "deep down my attitude is a protest against the fate that has made me a poet in an industrial age",[7] describes the forces at work inside the head of a modern poet: "He does not write for fame nor for money; he would be disappointed if he did. He merely writes to vent his own spleen, his own bitterness, his own sense of the disparity between the ugliness of the world that is and the beauty of the world that might be. He is trapped in a mechanical civilization. Everywhere about him are steel cages and the futile voices of slaves... to be part of civilization is to be part of its ugliness and haste and economic barbarism. It is to be a butterfly on the wheel. But a poet is born. He is born in spite of the civilization. When, therefore, he is born into this apathetic and hostile civilization, he will react in the only possible way, he will become the poet of his own spleen, the victim of his own frustrated sense of beauty, the prophet of despair".[8]

Here we can recognise the cry of rage of many a contemporary rebel, most obviously perhaps in the punk tradition. An age of harmony and beauty might produce music to match, but, for the punk or modern poet, it would be a betrayal of truth to pretend that this was the case today and to write sweet odes to love or nature. Born 1,000 years ago, 10,000 years ago, or maybe 100 years from now, that same individual could have been expressing something else entirely. But their authenticity, their honesty, demands that they voice what they feel and not what they would like to feel or what they think others might want them to voice. Here is the anarchist, in the rawness of discovering the falsity of all that surrounds them, in their rage at finding they are blocked from being what they are meant to be in the society of which they were meant to be part. Here is the stage of something close to nihilism that many of us go through, the descent into the fires of despair that can burn us up entirely but which, if we are able to survive it, leaves us hardened by the flames and ready to carry on at a new level. The screaming fury of the angry young rebel never stops echoing in the back of our heads, but we try to find a way to carry on living without either burying it, betraying it or fully succumbing to it, and we find the true poetry of the anarchist in the daily courage of being ourselves in spite of everything.

For an artist or an anarchist, being free as an individual is absolutely non-negotiable, the foundation of everything that we do, and yet, at the same time, there is the awareness we are serving some greater purpose. There is no contradiction here, for it is only by being free inside that we can allow the collective inspiration to flow through us and make itself manifest through our words, deeds, images or songs. As Carl Jung says: "Art is a kind of innate drive that seizes a human being and makes him its instrument. The artist is not a person endowed with free will who seeks his own ends, but one who allows art to realize its purposes through him".[9] Berman and Luke describe how Landauer sees human essence as residing in each individual as communal consciousness, or social individuality: "Art, music and poetry effectively can interpret this consciousness as a form of worldly understanding. Here, Landauer's life-long interest in poets of folk consciousness – Shakespeare in England, Whitman in the United States, or Hölderlin in Germany – illustrates his understanding of the folk spirit, as well as each individual poet's artistry, which articulates his social individuality. The poet, as in Whitman's 'Song of Myself', speaks not for his *own* self, but for his *folk* self, embedded in his individual consciousness, his language, culture, society, and communal order".[10]

Art and poetry are an expression of the social organism and have their source in the collective unconscious. "What is essential in a work of art is that it should rise far above the realm of personal life and speak from the spirit and heart of the poet as man to the spirit and heart of mankind",[11] says Jung. Art, as we saw in Chapter I, can reflect the negative aspects of contemporary reality – Oswald Spengler, for instance, identifies the art of our civilization as dead and artificial, with "no further organic future"[12] and John Ruskin in *The Mysteries of Life and Its Arts* similarly feels that to rediscover authenticity there is a need to "go back to the root of it, or, at least, to the place where the stock of it is yet alive, and the branches began to die".[13] But it can also act as an outlet for positive forces within the organism, not just in terms of the initial individual despair at the ways things are, but as a focus for the need for change.

All forms of art can re-activate the sense of spirituality that has faded so badly in the materialist age. Andrew Harvey, for instance, regards Rumi as "not only our supreme poet – but also an essential guide to the new mystical Renaissance that is struggling to be born against terrible odds in the rubble of our dying civilization",[14] and adds: "Returning mankind to a vision of the perfect human being as the goal of life is essential to the survival of the human race".[15] Robin Waterfield describes the arts as being "so constituted as to rejoice the souls of men, to raise, by means of their beauty, their spirits beyond the beauties of nature to the Divine Source of all beauty,"[16] and Jung sees hope for the future in "the useful and edifying models held up to us by poets and philosophers – models or *archetypi* that we may well call remedies for both men and the times".[17]

Creative individuals can also play a more direct role in setting the collective spirit moving in a certain direction, as Landauer observes when he says the spark for revolution is always the stupidity, brutality or weakness of rulers, but that "the people, the thinkers, the poets are a powder keg, loaded with spirit and the power of creative destruction".[18] If the revolutionary spirit is not in evidence, then this could be a reflection of the extent to which society, like religion (and anarchism?), is cutting itself off from its own vital inner inspiration. While poets and artists are certainly still held in esteem by society, their message is regarded as being for entertainment purposes only and kept separate from the "serious" business of determining how the material world is ordered, thus denying them their natural role in gently steering the collective consciousness in a healthy direction.

Read says that the ideal anarchist society requires organic unity, but to achieve this unity a culture is necessary and "there is no culture unless an intimate relationship, on the level of instinct, exists between a people and its poets".[19] The lack of this relationship, the futility of giving voice to the spirit of dissent in a materialist world that is just not listening, plunges the contemporary artist and poet further down the spiral of dark despair. What possible way out is there? There is a blockage here which seems to prevent any solution. The pragmatic, positivist, materialist, mindset which has successfully been imposed on the population precludes the imaginative thinking of the poet from being regarded as anything more than an irrelevant diversion and, as we have seen, closes down all possibilities of thinking outside the prescribed norms.

This blockage evidently needs to be cleared – Herbert Marcuse comments that the self-determination of a living society will only be real "to the extent to which the masses have been dissolved into individuals liberated from all propaganda, indoctrination, and manipulation, capable of knowing and comprehending the facts and of evaluating the alternatives".[20] But how could this be achieved? Marcuse suggests that "the mere absence of all advertising and all indoctrinating media of information and entertainment would plunge the individual into a traumatic void where he would have the chance to wonder and to think"[21] and that "the non-functioning of television and the allied media might thus begin to achieve what the inherent contradictions of capitalism did not achieve – the disintegration of the system".[22]

Whether this state of affairs would be the cause of the disintegration of the system or the result of it, is a matter for further consideration and the possibility is certainly not one we can rely on becoming a reality. What is urgently needed is a means of breaking through the indoctrination that closes people's minds to the messages of the artists and the anarchists and also keeps them apart from the collective soul buried within themselves. Waterfield says this process of recovering what people once knew will be slow since it "requires a commitment that goes far beyond intellectual assent and demands a *metanoia* or change of mind",[23] which he defines as "a total reorientation of one's whole being by means of a renewed committal to living the truth at no matter what cost".[24]

As we have seen regarding the use of paradox, a creative method is required to penetrate the trained defences of a socially obedient mind and sow the seed of this *metanoia*. Idries Shah points out that Sufis often present the same thought in many different forms in order to get it to sink in: "Sufis say that an idea will enter the conditioned (veiled) mind only if it is so phrased as to be able to bypass the screen of conditionings".[25] As poets know full well, the very language in which ideas are expressed has a heavy influence on the extent to which they can be successfully communicated. The evolution of modern language, and the loss of contact with original meanings, makes it easier for language to be misused and harder for it to be used to express concepts that don't form part of contemporary materialist discourse. By way of contrast, the ancient language of Sanskrit is based on 3,000 monosyllabic roots, each having a definite, almost physical meaning, explains Waterfield: "New compounds can be formed at will and in them the basic meanings of the syllables are preserved... In Sanskrit the range of spoken sounds has almost the regularity of a musical scale. It is a wonderful instrument for poetic utterance, the words themselves giving directly rise to images; no language is better suited to the description of nature".[26]

In the absence of an existing living language that can express the poetry of life in opposition to the death of our cancerous civilization, we must create one of our own, not just in words, but in pictures, music and in the very way we act and are. We need a language, in this loose sense, that can penetrate the veils of ignorance with which this culture hides itself from any truthful scrutiny and exposes the hypocrisy and tyranny of power and control. By envisaging the future existence we yearn for, and by contrasting it with the dire circumstances we find ourselves in today, we can at least begin the process by providing a foundation of general awareness. This can develop into the idea that the "should" is also a "could" and that another world is indeed possible, even if not immediately within our grasp. In itself, this represents a huge leap forward and one against which the contemporary conditioned mind has been well-prepared – the imagining of any reality other than existing reality is generally held to be fanciful to the point of laughable stupidity.

But our revolution of language and, thus, thought must take us much further yet. The next stage must be the conversion of dream into desire, the formulation – through the magic of art, poetry and all the beauty of the human soul that they express – of the definite wish for the possible new world to become reality, not in some far-off era but imminently. When the visionaries are also anarchists, it will not be a question of waiting for this image of a free and fulfilled future to be fully formed and living in the mind's eye of the people, before taking action – instead our resistance will be a part of our poetry as we bid our fellows come forward and seize, at last, what is rightfully ours.

XI

¡VIVA LA REVELACIÓN!

A remarkable transformation is required if we are to shake off the mental disease that is condemning humanity, and the planet, to a slow and ignoble death by ignorance and greed. An awakening is required on a scale never seen before, an awakening that will spread like a tsunami around the globe, sweeping away the machineries and mindset of hateful oppression and denial. It is not so much a revolution that is needed, but a revelation – a lifting of all the veils of falsity and a joyful rediscovery of the authentic core of our existence.

"Religion starts like a great shout," says Oswald Spengler. "Gloomy apprehension is suddenly dispelled by a fervid wakening that blossoms plantwise from mother earth and at one glance takes in the depth of the light-world. In this moment – never earlier, and never (at least with the same deep intensity) later – it traverses the chosen spirits of the time like a grand light, which dissolves all fear in blissful love and lets the invisible appear, all suddenly, in a metaphysical radiance".[1] This revelation is not going to come from one of the existing exoteric forms of religion which have exhausted their essential vitality, withered inside and become nothing more than vehicles of worldly power and control. Neither is it going to come from some newly fabricated imitation of religion, a shallow concoction of superficial characteristics of spirituality considered entertaining and harmless by the dominant system.

This new revelation must start from within the individual, from within the existential grasping of the need to *be* that is born of self-searching alienation and the burning away of the dross of the ego. But the alchemy of spiritual renewal will have to be a universal one, in which not just the microcosm of the individual but the macrocosm of the whole is purified and turned to gold. Furthermore, if this revelation is to be a true revelation, it will have to emerge from concealment – it will have to possess the primal power of discovery, even though what it reveals will be as old as time itself. Thus it is that Karl Jaspers urges "we do everything in our power to restore the eternal truth; we must plumb its very depths and, unconcerned over what is transcient and historical, utter this truth in a new language".[2]

And where is this new language of religion to come from? When Saul Newman suggests that "perhaps anarchism could become a new 'heroic' philosophy, which is no longer reactive but, rather, creates values",[3] he is pointing us towards the answer. The values of anarchism are "new" enough to force the massive changes for which the human soul is thirsting, but sink their roots into the deepest, richest soil of our collective psyche. This is the revelation we need – the Anarchist Revelation!

The religion behind this revelation – a glorious fusion of the earthly insurgent dynamic and the transcendent esoteric insight with which it is so eminently compatible – will not look like any religion that has been seen before. Gone will be all the outdated relics of what are today called religions, after we have asked ourselves, as Jaspers proposes, "which dogmas can be dropped because they have actually become alien to modern man and lost their credibility?"[4] When we understand that the essence of authentic spirituality is both universal and timeless, that it can assume all manner of forms and yet remain exactly what it always was, then we will be free to express our longing for truth in the way which is most appropriate to the age we live in and which will ensure the message is understood and embraced. Frithjof Schuon is quite clear on this point, when he declares: "If a new Revelation may thus justifiably depreciate traditional values of an earlier origin, it is because it is independent of these values and has no need of them, since it possesses equivalent values of its own and is therefore entirely self-sufficient".[5]

Anarchism has values of its own aplenty and its revelation is a contemporary rebirth of the primordial religion that was the origin of all other religions, before they atrophied. Martin Lings explains that Islam understands this universal primal beginning and "one of the characteristics of the Qur'an as the last Revelation is that at times it becomes as it were transparent in order that the first Revelation may shine through its verses; and this first Revelation, namely the Book of Nature, belongs to everyone".[6] This, too, is the quality of the Anarchist Revelation – it belongs to everyone and seeks to bring about a general transparency so that authentic truth can be revealed.

It reveals the sorry state of contemporary humanity: cut-off from reality, from others and the whole by the alienation of technology, of conformity, of conditioning. It reveals the falsity of our so-called democracy and exposes the destruction, the exploitation, the deceit, that hides behind it. It reveals the sick parody of justice, the outrageous theft of land, the intolerable denial of freedom that imprisons each and every one of us. It reveals how the lie of progress and the empty restrictive language of one-dimensional thinking are promoted by capitalism to close down our understanding of the world and have us think that there is no other possible reality.

The Anarchist Revelation shows us that this is not how things are *meant* to be; this is not how we are all *meant* to live – and it inspires us to put things right. It inspires us to fly free over the barriers erected around us, riding the winds of human passion and yearning. It inspires us to see that the state is a destroyer of life, not a necessity for it, and thus to kick over the whole house of cards of authority and control. It inspires us to draw on the energy flowing through ourselves, to find our *dharma* and to be guided by the "original instructions" and natural laws of organic self-governing society. It inspires us to plug ourselves back into the collective unconscious, into the heart of nature and to know that if we don't stop civilization from murdering the planet, nothing else matters. It inspires us to take our despair into ourselves and find the courage to exist, to understand that our glorious gift as individuals is to be the only means by which the collective spirit has an actual physical existence and to accept the noble burden of responsibility which this bestows upon us. It inspires us to let out a collective cry of courageous refusal and to know, above all, that the future is not yet written.

It is the Anarchist Revelation that will bring about the *metanoia* we need to fight off the cancer that is killing us. Have no doubt that the primal power of its light will prevail over the darkness. "As soon as the Ideal is put before mankind, all former ideals will fade away as the stars fade before the rising sun",[7] writes Leo Tolstoy. Neither, as Landauer observes, need we worry that the quantity of those answering the call will not be great enough, when the quality of its content is beyond question: "There is no need to fear a lack of revolutionaries: they actually arise by a sort of spontaneous generation – namely when the revolution comes... The voice of the spirit is the trumpet that will sound again and again and again, as long as men are together. Injustice will always seek to perpetuate itself; and always as long as men are truly alive, revolt against it will break out".[8]

Anarchy is not a dry theory, analysis or programme, but a manifestation – in the realm of ideas – of the life-force itself, the *Tao* that has been blocked by the capitalist death-system. As such, it can never be crushed, recuperated or forgotten. It lives on in the blood of each new generation of humanity, reborn again and again, becoming stronger and stronger the more its destiny is denied. "The living spirit grows and even outgrows its earlier forms of expression; it freely chooses the men in whom it lives and who proclaim it," writes Carl Jung. "This living spirit is eternally renewed and pursues its goal in manifold and inconceivable ways throughout the history of mankind. Measured against it, the names and forms which men have given it mean little enough; they are only the changing leaves and blossoms on the stem of the eternal tree".[9]

Once the Anarchist Revelation has achieved its transformative purpose it will no longer have to maintain the same shape and will not need the hard anger of revolt; organic society will no longer have to throw up men and women destined to incarnate that rebellion; individuals of a particular kind will no longer find themselves to be outsiders and rebels impelled to dedicate their lives to lonely defiance and bitter resistance. We will have reached *eudaimonia:*[10] we will be living the way we are meant to live in the earthy tangle of nature, the perfect imperfection of what is real and true and growing. And our primal religion will remind us that, as the *Hermetica* say: "All things are linked together, and connected one with another in a chain extending from the lowest to the highest; so that we see that they are not many, or rather, that all are one".[11]

ENDNOTES

I

A World Gone Mad

1. Herbert Marcuse, *One Dimensional Man: Studies in the Ideology of Advanced Industrial Society*, (London: Routledge & Kegan Paul, 1964) p. 183.
2. Derrick Jensen, *Endgame, Vol 1: The Problem of Civilization*, (New York: Seven Stories Press, 2006) p. 151.
3. "Vous n'avez plus droit à ce qu'on peut appeler une solitude créatrice. Le vertige que procure les outils techniques comme le portable empêche l'individu d'exister par lui-même". *La réalité unique, nouvelle idéologie: Entretien avec François Brune* in *Divertir pour dominer: La culture de masse contre les peuples,* (Montreuil: Editions L'Echappée, 2010) pp. 87-88.
4. "La magie de l'écran est une communication à sens unique... La télé, c'est la vie confisquée". *L'âge de la télévision: Entretien avec Jean-Jacques Wunenburger* in *Divertir pour dominer: La culture de masse contre les peuples*, p. 41.
5. "Je ne suis plus moi-même lorsque je regarde la télévision, ma conscience se plaque sur le flux d'images: je deviens ce que je regarde". Guillaume Carnino, *Une aliénation de la conscience* in *Divertir pour dominer: La culture de masse contre les peuples*, p. 43.
6. "La télévision est donc une aliénation (au sens étymologique, l'aliénation n'est rien d'autre que le fait de se "rendre étranger" à soi-même, d'être "dépossédé" de soi): lorsqu'on la regarde on échappe à ses pensées, on s'échappe à soi-même". Guillaume Carnino, *Une aliénation de la conscience* in *Divertir pour dominer: La culture de masse contre les peuples*, pp. 43-44.
7. Joseph Campbell, *The Hero With a Thousand Faces,* (London: Fontana Press, 1993) p. 216.
8. Aldous Huxley, *The Perennial Philosophy*, (London: Chatto & Windus, 1980) p. 250.
9. "Nos émissions ont pour vocation de le rendre disponible [le cerveau du téléspectateur], c'est-à-dire de le divertir, de le détendre pour le préparer

entre deux messages. Ce que nous vendons à Coca-Cola, c'est du temps de cerveau humain disponible." Sophie Pietrucci, Chris Vientiane and Aude Vincent, *Contre les publicités sexistes* (Montreuil: Editions L'Echappée, 2012) p. 15.

10. "C'est un totalitarisme. Ce qui le différencie des totalitarismes d'antan, c'est qu'il est moins brutal mais beaucoup plus insidieux. Comme le disait Aldous Huxley, le principe de la stabilité sociale consiste à faire désirer aux gens ce qu'on a programmé pour eux. C'est exactement ce que fait la publicité." *La réalité unique, nouvelle idéologie: Entretien avec François Brune* in *Divertir pour dominer: La culture de masse contre les peuples*, p. 89.

11. Gustav Landauer, *For Socialism*, trans. by David J Parent, (St Louis: Telos Press, 1978) pp. 35-36.

12. Kit Pedler, *The Quest for Gaia: A Book of Changes*, (London: Granada, 1981) p. 68.

13. "L'avoir, et non plus l'être, devient l'unique source de désir". Guillaume Carnino, *Le contrôle par la consommation* in *Divertir pour dominer: La culture de masse contre les peuples*, p. 105.

14. Jean Baudrillard, *La société de consommation, ses mythes, ses structures*, (Paris: Folio, 2011) p. 176.

15. George Woodcock, *Herbert Read: The Stream and the Source*, (Montreal/New York/London: Black Rose Books, 2008) p. 202.

16. Hermann Hesse, *Steppenwolf*, (London: Penguin, 2011) p. 177.

17. Friedrich Nietzsche, *The Will to Power*, in *Existentialism from Dostoevsky to Sartre*, ed. by Walter Kaufmann, (New York: Meridian, 1972) p. 110.

18. René Guénon, *The Crisis of the Modern World*, trans. by Arthur Osborne, Marco Pallis and Richard C Nicholson, (Ghent NY: Sophia Perennis, 2001) p. 50.

19. René Guénon, *East and West*, trans. by Martin Lings, (Hillsdale NY: Sophia Perennis, 2004) p. 60.

20. Marcuse, p. 95.

21. "Plus de transcendance, plus de finalité, plus d'objectif: ce qui caractérise cette société, c'est l'absence de 'réflexion', de perspective sur elle-même". Baudrillard, p. 309.

22. Derrick Jensen, *Dreams,* (New York: Seven Stories Press, 2011) p. 215.

23. Karl Jaspers, *Man in the Modern Age,* trans. by Eden and Cedar Paul, (London: Routledge & Kegan Paul, 1951) p. 120.

24. "Il y a aujourd'hui tout autour de nous une espèce d'évidence fantastique de la consommation et de l'abondance, constituée par la multiplication des objets, des services, des biens matériels, et qui constitue une sorte de mutation fondamentale dans l'écologie de l'espèce humaine. A proprement parler, les hommes de l'opulence ne sont plus tellement environnés, comme ils le furent de tout temps, par d'autres hommes que par des OBJETS". Baudrillard, p. 17.

25. *"Toute chose produite est sacralisée par le fait même de l'être.* Toute chose

produite est positive, toute chose mesurable est positive". Baudrillard, p. 46.

II

Freedom Obstructed

1. Joseph Campbell, *The Masks of God: Oriental Mythology*, (London: Secker & Warburg, 1962) p. 112.

2. Colin Wilson, *The Outsider*, (London: Victor Gollancz, 1956) p. 260.

3. "Car dans un même mouvement, le capitalisme désenchante le monde, détruit toute forme d'authenticité, d'autonomie et de créativité et engendre des inégalités croissantes en favorisant les intérêts d'une minorité." *Divertir pour dominer: La culture de masse contre les peuples,* (Montreuil: Editions L'Echappée, 2010) p. 14.

4. Oswald Spengler, *The Decline of the West,* (Oxford: Oxford University Press, 1991) p. 24.

5. Herbert Read, *The Contrary Experience*, cit. George Woodcock, *Herbert Read: The Stream and the Source,* (Montreal/New York/London: Black Rose Books, 2008) p. 53.

6. Derrick Jensen, *Endgame Vol I: The Problem of Civilization,* (New York: Seven Stories Press, 2006) p. 231.

7. John Zerzan, *Running on Emptiness: The Pathology of Civilization,* (Los Angeles: Feral House, 2002) p. 78.

8. René Guénon, *The Crisis of the Modern World*, trans. by Arthur Osborne, Marco Pallis and Richard C Nicholson, (Ghent NY: Sophia Perennis, 2001) p. 19.

9. Mark Sedgwick, *Against the Modern World: Traditionalism and the Secret Intellectual History of the Twentieth Century,* (New York: Oxford University Press, 2009) p. 21.

10. Sedgwick, p. 34.

11. Karl Jaspers, *Man in the Modern Age,* trans. by Eden and Cedar Paul, (London: Routledge & Kegan Paul, 1951) pp. 110-11.

12. Aldous Huxley, *The Perennial Philosophy,* (London: Chatto & Windus, 1980), p. 82.

13. John Zerzan, *Future Primitive and Other Essays*, (Camberley: Green Anarchist Books, 1996), p. 138.

14. CG Jung, *Symbols of Transformation,* trans. by R.F.C Hull (Princeton NJ: Princeton University Press, 1990), p. 178.

15. Spengler, p. 250.

16. Jung, *Symbols of Transformation*, p. 202.

17. Leo Tolstoy, *A Calendar of Wisdom,* (London: Hodder & Stoughton, 1998) p. 321.

18. Idries Shah, *The Sufis,* (London: WH Allen & Co 1977) p. 332.

19. Harry R Moody and David Carroll, *The Five Stages of The Soul: Charting the Spiritual Passages That Shape Our Lives*, (London: Rider, 1999) p. 126.

20. June Singer, *The Unholy Bible: Blake, Jung and the Collective Unconscious.* (Boston, USA: Sigo Press, 1986) p. 94.

21. Huxley, p. 176.

22. Baruch de Spinoza, *Ethics*, 4, 24, cit. Roger Scruton, *Spinoza: A Very Short Introduction*, (Oxford: Oxford University Press, 2002), p. 90.

23. Friedrich Nietzsche, *The Genealogy of Morals*, cit. Max Cafard, *Nietzschean Anarchy and the Post-Mortem Condition* in *I Am Not A Man, I Am Dynamite: Friedrich Nietzsche and the Anarchist Tradition*, ed. by John Moore with Spencer Sunshine, (Brooklyn, New York: Autonomedia, 2004) p. 98.

24. Spengler, p. 72.

25. Derrick Jensen, *Dreams* (New York: Seven Stories Press, 2011), p. 445.

26. Woodcock, *Herbert Read: The Stream and the Source,* p. 246.

27. Jung, *Symbols of Transformation,* p. 158.

28. CG Jung, *Modern Man In Search of A Soul,* (London: Routledge & Kegan Paul, 1978) pp. 129-30.

29. Jung, *Modern Man In Search of A Soul,* p. 130.

30. Jung, *Symbols of Transformation,* p. 77.

31. Jung, *Modern Man in Search of a Soul,* p. 216.

32. Jung, *Modern Man in Search of a Soul,* p. 215.

33. Joseph Campbell, *The Hero With a Thousand Faces,* (London: Fontana Press, 1993) pp. 17-18.

34. Campbell, *The Hero With a Thousand Faces,* p. 4.

35. John Ruskin, *Athena Keramitis* in *The Genius of John Ruskin: Selections from his Writings,* ed. by John D Rosenberg (London: George Allen & Unwin Ltd, 1964) p. 358.

36. Murray Stein, *In Midlife: A Jungian Perspective*, (Dallas: Spring Publications, 1983) p. 112.

37. Stein, p. 113.

38. Frithjof Schuon, *The Transcendent Unity of Religions,* trans. by Peter Townsend, (London: Faber & Faber, 1953) p. 93.

39. CG Jung, *The Soul and Death* in *Structure and Dynamics of the Psyche,* cit. June Singer, *The Unholy Bible: Blake, Jung and the Collective Unconscious,* p. 168.

40. CG Jung, *Psychology and Alchemy*, (London: Routledge, 1989) p. 137.

41. Jung, *Modern Man In Search of A Soul,* p 142.

42. Campbell, *The Hero With a Thousand Faces,* p. 11.

43. Paul Shepard, *Nature and Madness*, (Athens, USA: University of Georgia Press, 1998) p. 6.

44. Shepard, p. 109.

45. Shepard, p. 66.

46. Eugène N Marais, *The Soul of the White Ant*, (London: Jonathan Cape

and Anthony Blond, 1971) pp. 17-20.

47. Shepard, p. 16.

48. RD Laing, *The Politics of Experience,* (New York: Ballantine, 1967) cit. Derrick Jensen, *Endgame Vol I: The Problem of Civilization,* (New York: Seven Stories Press, 2006) pp. 38-39.

49. Lieh Tzu, cit. Joseph Campbell, *The Masks of God: Oriental Mythology,* (London: Secker & Warburg, 1962) p. 436.

50. Herbert Read, *The Philosophy of Anarchism,* cit. Woodcock, *Herbert Read: The Stream and the Source,* p. 192.

51. René Guénon, *The Reign of Quantity and the Signs of the Times,* trans. by Lord Northbourne, (Hillsdale NY, Sophia Perennis, 2004) p. 43.

III

Dump the System!

1. Oswald Spengler, *The Decline of the West,* (Oxford: Oxford University Press, 1991) p. 17.

2. Spengler, p. 18.

3. Spengler, p. 28.

4. Spengler, p. 187.

5. Spengler, p.5.

6. Spengler, p. 75.

7. Joseph Campbell, *The Hero With a Thousand Faces,* (London: Fontana Press, 1993) p. 266.

8. René Guénon, *The Crisis of the Modern World,* trans. by Arthur Osborne, Marco Pallis and Richard C Nicholson, (Ghent NY: Sophia Perennis, 2001) p. 17.

9. Herbert Read, *Poetry and Anarchism,* cit George Woodcock, *Herbert Read: The Stream and the Source* (Montreal/New York/London: Black Rose Books, 2008) p. 214.

10. Guénon, *The Crisis of the Modern World,* p. 2.

11. Guénon, *The Crisis of the Modern World,* p. 39.

12. John Ruskin, *Modern Manufacture and Design,* in *The Genius of John Ruskin: Selections from his Writings,* ed. by John D Rosenberg, (London: George Allen & Unwin Ltd, 1964) p. 223.

13. Herbert Read, cit. Woodcock, *Herbert Read: The Stream and the Source,* p. 232.

14. Anti-Authoritarians Anonymous, *We Have to Dismantle All This,* in *Against Civilization: Readings and Reflections,* ed. by John Zerzan, (Eugene, Oregon: Uncivilized Books, 1999) pp. 207-08.

15. David Watson, *Against The Megamachine: Essays on Empire and Its Enemies,* (Brooklyn, NY: Autonomedia, 1998) p. 197.

16. Kirkpatrick Sale, *After Eden: The Evolution of Human Domination*, (Durham and London: Duke University Press, 2006) p. 3.

17. Derrick Jensen and Aric McBay, *What We Leave Behind*, (New York: Seven Stories Press, 2009) p. 292.

18. Jensen and McBay, p. 101.

19. Jensen and McBay, p. 293.

20. Jensen and McBay, p. 101.

21. Richard Heinberg, *"Was Civilization A Mistake?"* in *Against Civilization: Readings and Reflections*, p. 103.

22. Derrick Jensen, *Dreams*, (New York: Seven Stories Press, 2011) p. 320.

23. Spengler, p. 411.

24. Sale, p. 3.

25. Jensen, *Dreams*, p. 26.

26. Jensen, *Dreams*, p. 249.

27. Guénon, *The Crisis of the Modern World*, p. 17.

28. René Guénon, *The Reign of Quantity and the Signs of the Times*, trans. by Lord Northbourne, (Hillsdale NY: Sophia Perennis, 2004) p. 163 (footnote).

29. Jensen, *Dreams*, p. 221.

30. Unabomber (AKA 'FC'), *Industrial Society and Its Future* in *Against Civilization: Readings and Reflections*, p. 119.

IV

The Lie of Democracy

1. Pierre-Joseph Proudhon, cit. Peter Marshall, *Demanding the Impossible: A History of Anarchism*, (London: Fontana Press, 1993) p. 244.

2. Michael Bakunin, *Oeuvres*, Vol II, 1907, in *The Anarchist Reader,* ed. by George Woodcock, (Glasgow: Fontana, 1986) p. 108.

3. René Guénon, *The Crisis of the Modern World*, trans. by Arthur Osborne, Marco Pallis and Richard C Nicholson, (Ghent NY: Sophia Perennis, 2001) p. 74.

4. Oswald Spengler, *The Decline of the West* (Oxford: Oxford University Press, 1991) pp. 366-67.

5. Spengler, p. 391.

6. Speech at the White House, 1962.

7. http://www.eco-action.org/porkbolter/feb11.html.

8. Tom Anderson, *Infiltrated, Intimidated and Undermined: How Police Infiltration Can Mute Political Dissent, An Interview With Verity Smith from Cardiff Anarchist Network* in *Managing Democracy, Managing Dissent: Capitalism, Democracy and the Organisation of Consent*, ed. by Rebecca Fisher (London: Corporate Watch, 2013), p. 276.

9. http://policespiesoutoflives.org.uk.

10. Martin Ingram & Greg Harkin, *Stakeknife – Britain's Secret Agents in*

Ireland (Dublin: O'Brien Press, 2004).

http://www.guardian.co.uk/uk/2012/dec/12/pat-finucane-de-silva-report.

http://www.britisharmykillings.org.uk/product/468-50/Brian-Nelson.

11. Daniele Ganser, *Nato's Secret Armies: Operation Gladio and Terrorism in Western Europe* (London: Cass, 2005).

http://www.eco-action.org/porkbolter/gladio.html.

12. Seumas Milne, *The Enemy Within: Thatcher's Secret War Against the Miners*, (London: Verso, 2004).

13. Tom Anderson, *When Co-Option Fails* in *Managing Democracy, Managing Dissent: Capitalism, Democracy and the Organisation of Consent*, pp. 240-43.

14. Herbert Marcuse, *One Dimensional Man: Studies in the Ideology of Advanced Industrial Society*, (London: Routledge & Kegan Paul, 1964) p. 256.

15. http://www.medialens.org.

David Edwards and David Cromwell, *Guardians of Power: The Myth of the Liberal Media*, (London: Pluto, 2005).

David Edwards and David Cromwell, *Newspeak in the 21st Century*, (London: Pluto, 2009).

16. Edward S Herman and Noam Chomsky, *Manufacturing Consent: The Political Economy of the Mass Media,* (New York: Pantheon, 2002) p. 1.

17. Herman and Chomsky, p. 2.

18. Ibid.

19. Sharon Beder, *Global Spin: The Corporate Assault on Environmentalism,* (Totnes: Green Books, 2002) p. 275.

20. Beder, p. 276.

21. Beder, pp. 278-79.

22. Beder, p. 281.

23. Beder, pp. 282-83.

24. Derrick Jensen, *Endgame, Vol 1: The Problem of Civilization*, (New York: Seven Stories Press, 2006) pp. 200-01.

25. René Guénon, *East and West*, trans. by Martin Lings, (Hillsdale NY: Sophia Perennis, 2004) p. 15.

26. "Pour des millions de gens sans histoire, et heureux de l'être, il faut déculpabiliser la passivité". Jean Baudrillard, *La société de consommation, ses mythes, ses structures*, (Paris: Folio, 2011) p. 34.

27. "La vérité des media de masse est donc celle-ci: ils ont pour fonction de neutraliser le caractère vécu, unique, événementiel du monde, pour substituer un univers multiple de media homogènes les uns aux autres en tant que tels, se signifiant l'un l'autre et renvoyant les uns aux autres. A la limite, ils deviennent le contenu réciproque les uns des autres – et c'est là *le "message" totalitaire d'une société de consommation*." Baudrillard, p. 189.

28. "Espérer être libre implique déjà d'avoir conscience de ses chaînes, et non de vivre comme si elles n'existaient pas." Guillaume Carnino, *Choisir ou être libre* in *Divertir pour dominer: La culture de masse contre les peuples,* (Montreuil: Editions L'Echappée, 2010) p 129.

29. Colin Wilson, *The Outsider*, (London: Victor Gollancz, 1956) p. 195.

30. Marcuse, pp. 88-91.

31. Marcuse, p. 104.

32. Spengler, p. 395.

33. Guénon, *The Crisis of the Modern World*, p. 66.

34. Marcuse, p.172.

35. See Chapter 1, Endnote 21.

36. Karl Jaspers, *Man in the Modern Age*, (London: Routledge & Kegan Paul, 1951) p. 50.

37. Guénon, *East and West*, p 53.

38. Guénon, *East and West*, p. 38.

39. Robert Ardrey, *Introduction*, Eugène Marais, *The Soul of the Ape*, (London: Anthony Blond Ltd, 1969) pp. 30-31.

40. Stanley Aronowitz, cit. Derrick Jensen, *Dreams*, (New York: Seven Stories Press, 2011) p138.

41. Marcuse, p. 158.

V

Anarchy is Life

1. Leo Tolstoy, *The Slavery of Our Times*, 1900, in *The Anarchist Reader,* ed. by George Woodcock, (Glasgow: Fontana, 1986) p. 118.

2. Alexander Berkman, *What is Anarchist Communism?*, 1929, in *The Anarchist Reader*, pp. 185-86.

3. Michael Bakunin, *The Knouto-Germanic Empire and the Social Revolution*, in *The Political Philosophy of Bakunin: Scientific Anarchism*, ed. by G.P. Maximoff, (New York: The Free Press of Glencoe, 1964) p. 241.

4. Emile Henry, *Gazette des Tribunaux*, 27-28 April 1894, in *The Anarchist Reader,* pp. 190-91.

5. William Godwin, *Enquiry Concerning Political Justice*, 1793, in *The Anarchist Reader,* p. 131.

6. Pierre-Joseph Proudhon, *What Is Property?*, cit. George Woodcock, *Anarchism*, (London: Penguin, 1979) p. 105.

7. Gustav Landauer, *For Socialism*, trans. by David J Parent, (St Louis: Telos Press, 1978) p. 128.

8. Michael Bakunin, *Philosophical Considerations*, in *The Political Philosophy of Bakunin: Scientific Anarchism*, p. 188.

9. Errico Malatesta, *Anarchy*, 1906, in *The Anarchist Reader,* pp. 63-64.

10. George Woodcock, *The Rejection of Politics*, 1972, in *The Anarchist Reader,* pp. 132-36.

11. Michael Bakunin, *Statism and Anarchism*, in *The Political Philosophy of Bakunin: Scientific Anarchism*, p. 60.

12. Bakunin, *The Knouto-Germanic Empire and the Social Revolution*, in *The Political Philosophy of Bakunin: Scientific Anarchism*, p. 77.
13. Gustav Landauer, *Revolution and Other Writings: A Political Reader*, ed. and trans. by Gabriel Kuhn, (Oakland: PM Press, 2010) p. 74.
14. Emma Goldman, *The Place of the Individual in Society*, 1940, cit. Peter Marshall, *Demanding the Impossible: A History of Anarchism,* (London: Fontana Press, 1993) p. 403.
15. Landauer, *Revolution and Other Writings: A Political Reader*, p. 22.
16. Peter Kropotkin, *Mutual Aid: A Factor of Evolution*, (London: Freedom Press, 1993) p. 180.
17. Michael Bakunin, *Federalism, Socialism and Anti-Theologism*, in *The Political Philosophy of Bakunin: Scientific Anarchism*, p. 55.
18. Bakunin, *The Knouto-Germanic Empire and the Social Revolution*, in *The Political Philosophy of Bakunin: Scientific Anarchism*, p. 239.
19. Woodcock, *The Anarchist Reader*, p. 12.
20. Pierre-Joseph Proudhon, *De la justice dans la révolution et dans l'église*, in *The Anarchist Reader,* p. 20.
21. Landauer, *Revolution and Other Writings: A Political Reader*, p. 170.
22. Herbert Marcuse, *One Dimensional Man: Studies in the Ideology of Advanced Industrial Society*, (London: Routledge & Kegan Paul, 1964) pp. 256-57.
23. Henry, *Gazette des Tribunaux*, 27-28 April 1894 in *The Anarchist Reader,* p. 196.

VI

The Courage to Exist

1. Hermann Hesse, *Remembrance of Hans*, cit. Ralph Freedman, *Hermann Hesse: Pilgrim of Crisis*, (London: Abacus, 1981) pp. 194-95.
2. Colin Wilson, *The Outsider*, (London: Victor Gollancz, 1956) p. 113.
3. René Guénon, *The Reign of Quantity and the Signs of the Times*, trans. by Lord Northbourne, (Hillsdale NY: Sophia Perennis, 2004) p. 106.
4. John Ruskin, *The Catholic Prayer*, in *The Genius of John Ruskin: Selections from his Writings,* ed. by John D Rosenberg, (London, George Allen & Unwin Ltd, 1964) p. 417.
5. Colin Wilson, *Religion and the Rebel*, (London: Victor Gollancz, 1957) p. 178.
6. Wilson, *The Outsider*, p. 84.
7. Paul Tillich, *The Courage To Be*, (London and Glasgow: Fontana, 1973) p. 71.
8. Jean-Paul Sartre, *Existentialism is a Humanism*, in *Existentialism from Dostoevsky to Sartre,* ed. by Walter Kaufmann, (New York: Meridian, 1972) p. 291.

9. Karl Jaspers, *Man in the Modern Age,* trans. by Eden and Cedar Paul, (London: Routledge & Kegan Paul, 1951) p. 128.
10. Jaspers, *Man in the Modern Age,* pp. 144-45.
11. Wilson, *Religion and the Rebel,* p. 104.
12. George Steiner, *In Bluebeard's Castle,* p. 19, cit. Paul Shepard, *Nature and Madness,* (Athens, USA: University of Georgia Press, 1998) p. 151.
13. Murray Stein, *In Midlife: A Jungian Perspective,* (Dallas: Spring Publications, 1983) pp. 124-25.
14. CG Jung, *Psychology and Alchemy,* (London: Routledge, 1989) p. 30 (footnote).
15. Wilson, *Religion and the Rebel,* p. 317.
16. Jaspers, *Man in the Modern Age,* p. 145.
17. Jaspers, *Man in the Modern Age,* pp. 176-77.

VII

Our Spirit is Universal!

1. Derrick Jensen, *Dreams,* (New York: Seven Stories Press, 2011) p. 319.
2. Jensen, *Dreams,* p. 274.
3. Colin Wilson, *Religion and the Rebel,* (London: Victor Gollancz, 1957) p. 9.
4. Wilson, *Religion and the Rebel,* p. 104.
5. John Ruskin, *Of Kings' Treasuries* in *The Genius of John Ruskin: Selections from his Writings,* ed. by John D Rosenberg, (London, George Allen & Unwin Ltd, 1964) p. 312.
6. Karl Jaspers, *Drives to the Basic Question,* in *Existentialism from Dostoevsky to Sartre,* ed. by Walter Kaufmann, (New York: Meridian, 1972) p. 138.
7. Margaret Smith, *The Way of the Mystics: The Early Christian Mystics and the Rise of the Sufis,* (London: Sheldon Press, 1976) p. 2.
8. Ibn 'Arabi, cit. Reynold A Nicholson, *The Mystics of Islam,* (London: Routledge & Kegan Paul, 1979) pp. 87-88.
9. Idries Shah, *The Sufis,* (London: WH Allen & Co, 1977) p. 25.
10. Ibn 'Arabi, *Kitab al-isra,* cit. Michel Chodkiewicz, *Introduction,* Ibn Al-Husayn Al-Sulami, *The Book of Sufi Chivalry: Lessons to a Son of the Moment, Futuwwah,* (London, East West Publications, 1983) p. 24.
11. Andrew Harvey, *The Way of Passion: A Celebration of Rumi,* (New York: Jeremy P Tarcher/Putnam, 2001) p. 248.
12. Hermann Hesse, *Steppenwolf,* (London: Penguin, 2011) p. 76.
13. Smith, p. 85.
14. Nicholson, p. 167.
15. Smith, p. 216.
16. Chodkiewicz, *Introduction,* Ibn Al-Husayn Al-Sulami, *The Book of Sufi Chivalry: Lessons to a Son of the Moment, Futuwwah,* p. 22.

17. Paul Tillich, *The Courage to Be,* (London and Glasgow: Fontana, 1973) p. 168.

18. *Rumi's Discourses,* cit. Harvey, p. 248.

19. René Guénon, *East and West,* trans. by Martin Lings, (Hillsdale NY: Sophia Perennis, 2004) p. 123.

20. CG Jung, *Dreams,* (London: Routledge, 2002) p. 80.

21. Andrew Harvey, *The Way of Passion: A Celebration of Rumi,* (New York: Jeremy P Tarcher/Putnam, 2001) pp. 268-69.

22. Robin Waterfield, *René Guénon and The Future of the West: The life and writings of a 20th-century metaphysician,* (Wellingborough: Crucible, 1987) p. 35.

23. Waterfield, pp. 37-38.

24. Mark Sedgwick, *Against the Modern World: Traditionalism and the Secret Intellectual History of the Twentieth Century,* (New York: Oxford University Press, 2009) pp. 45-48.

25. Sedgwick, p. 60.

26. Sedgwick, p. 61.

27. Ibid.

28. Sedgwick, pp. 62-63.

29. Waterfield, p. 40.

30. Waterfield, p. 41.

31. Ibid.

32. Waterfield, p. 42.

33. Waterfield, p. 153.

34. Sedgwick, p 34.

35. Alan Antliff, *Revolutionary Seer for Post-Industrial Age: Ananda Coomaraswamy's Nietzsche* in *I Am Not A Man, I Am Dynamite: Friedrich Nietzsche and the Anarchist Tradition,* ed. by John Moore with Spencer Sunshine, (Brooklyn, New York: Autonomedia, 2004) p. 46.

36. Sedgwick, p. 123.

37. Sedgwick, p. 149.

38. Peter Lamborn Wilson, *Crazy Nietzsche,* in *I Am Not A Man, I Am Dynamite: Friedrich Nietzsche and the Anarchist Tradition,* p. 147.

39. Peter Marshall, *Demanding the Impossible: A History of Anarchism,* (London: Fontana Press, 1993) p. 4.

40. Peter Marshall, *Riding the Wind: A New Philosophy for a New Era,* (London: Continuum, 2000) p. 16.

41. Marshall, *Riding the Wind: A New Philosophy for a New Era,* p. 8.

42. Herbert Read, *The Contrary Experience,* cit. George Woodcock, *Herbert Read: The Stream and the Source,* (Montreal/New York/London: Black Rose Books, 2008) pp. 50-51.

43. René Guénon, *The Crisis of the Modern World,* trans. by Arthur Osborne, Marco Pallis and Richard C Nicholson, (Ghent NY: Sophia Perennis, 2001) p. 98.

44. Stephan A Hoeller, *The Gnostic Jung and the Seven Sermons to the Dead,* (Wheaton IL: Quest, 1994) p. 14.

45. CG Jung, *Psychology and Alchemy,* (London: Routledge, 1989) p.102.

46. Margaret Smith, *The Way of the Mystics: The Early Christian Mystics and the Rise of the Sufis,* (London: Sheldon Press, 1976) p. 12.

47. Shah, p. 349.

48. Muqaddem 'Abd al-Qadir as-Sufi, *Introduction: Sufism Today,* in *The Tawasin of Mansur Al-Hallaj,* trans. by Aisha Abd Ar-Rahman At-Tarjumana, (Berkeley and London: Dirwana Press, 1974) p. 5.

49. William Blake, *The Marriage of Heaven and Hell,* cit. June Singer, *The Unholy Bible: Blake, Jung and the Collective Unconscious,* (Boston, USA: Sigo Press, 1986) p. 137.

50. *Notes from the Commentary of 'Abdul-Karim Jili* in Ibn 'Arabi, *Journey to the Lord of Power,* (London and The Hague: East West Publications, 1981) p. 103.

51. Ibid.

52. Shah, p. 72.

53. Patrick Harpur, *Mercurius: The Marriage of Heaven and Earth,* (Glastonbury: The Squeeze Press, 2008) p. 349.

54. Karl Jaspers, *Making Tradition Our Own,* in *Existentialism from Dostoevsky to Sartre,* p. 136.

55. Karl Jaspers, *Man in the Modern Age,* trans. by Eden and Cedar Paul, (London: Routledge & Kegan Paul, 1951) p. 178.

56. Frithjof Schuon, *The Transcendent Unity of Religions,* trans. by Peter Townsend, (London: Faber & Faber, 1953) p. 66.

57. Jean-Paul Sartre, *Existentialism is a Humanism,* in *Existentialism from Dostoevsky to Sartre,* p. 300.

58. Wilson, *Religion and the Rebel,* p. 151.

59. Herbert Read, *The Philosophy of Anarchism,* cit. Woodcock, *Herbert Read: The Stream and the Source,* p. 197.

60. Michael Bakunin, *Philosophical Considerations,* in G.P. Maximoff, *The Political Philosophy of Bakunin: Scientific Anarchism,* (New York: The Free Press of Glencoe, 1964) p. 53.

61. Russell Berman and Tim Luke, *Introduction,* Gustav Landauer, *For Socialism,* trans. by David J Parent, (St Louis: Telos Press, 1978) p. 4.

62. *Libellus X,* in *Hermetica: The Ancient Greek and Latin Writings Which Contain Religious or Philosophical Teachings Ascribed to Hermes Trismegistus,* ed. and trans. by Walter Scott, (Shaftesbury: Solos Press, 1997) p. 79.

63. Gustav Landauer, *Skepsis und Mystik: Versuche im Anschluss an Mauthners Sprachkritik,* (Cologne: 2d ed, 1923) p. 7, cit. Charles B Maurer, *Call to Revolution. The Mystical Anarchism of Gustav Landauer,* (Detroit: Wayne State University Press, 1971) p. 69.

VIII

Cleansing Fires of Revolution

1. CG Jung, *Psychology and Alchemy,* (London: Routledge, 1989) p. 471.

2. Robin Waterfield, *René Guénon and The Future of the West: The life and writings of a 20th-century metaphysician,* (Wellingborough: Crucible, 1987) pp. 118-19.

3. Gustav Meyrink, *The Angel of the West Window,* (Sawtry, Cambs: Dedalus, 1999) pp. 54-55.

4. June Singer, *The Unholy Bible: Blake, Jung and the Collective Unconscious,* (Boston, USA: Sigo Press, 1986) p. 76.

5. Margaret Smith, *The Way of the Mystics: The Early Christian Mystics and the Rise of the Sufis,* (London: Sheldon Press, 1976) p. 62.

6. Smith, p. 64.

7. John of Lycopolis, *The Spiritual State of the Soul,* Syriac Text, ed. by A Wensinck, (Amsterdam: 1923) xii, fol. 114*b*, cit. Smith, p. 92.

8. Smith, p. 92 (footnote).

9. Smith, p. 118.

10. Ibn Jawziya, cit. Tosun Bayrak al-Jerrahi, *Glimpses of the Life of Ibn 'Arabi,* in Ibn 'Arabi, *Journey to the Lord of Power,* (London and The Hague: East West Publications, 1981), p.16.

11. W.H.T. Gairdner, *"The Way" of a Mohammedan Mystic,* (Leipzig, 1912) pp. 9f cit. Reynold A Nicholson, *The Mystics of Islam,* (London: Routledge & Kegan Paul, 1979) pp. 15-16.

12. CG Jung, *Psychology and Alchemy,* (London: Routledge, 1989) pp. 99-100.

13. Jung, *Psychology and Alchemy,* pp. 304-06.

14. Jung, *Psychology and Alchemy,* pp. 427-28.

15. Jung, *Psychology and Alchemy,* p. 304.

16. Idries Shah, *The Sufis,* (London: WH Allen & Co, 1977) p. 199.

17. See Chapter VI.

18. Shah, p. 24.

19. Shah, p. 194.

20. Sufi dictum from the *Introduction to the Perception of Jafar Sadiq,* cit. Shah, p. 198.

21. Orthelius, *Epilogus et recapitulatio Orthelii,* cit. Jung, *Psychology and Alchemy,* p. 430.

22. Stephan A Hoeller, *The Gnostic Jung and the Seven Sermons to the Dead,* (Wheaton IL: Quest, 1994) p. 175.

23. Peter Marshall, *The Philosopher's Stone: A Quest for the Secrets of Alchemy,* (London: Pan Books, 2002) p. 461.

24. Gustav Landauer, *Revolution and Other Writings: A Political Reader,* ed. by Gabriel Kuhn, (Oakland: PM Press, 2010) p. 304.

25. Michael Bakunin, *Appeal to the Slavs,* cit. George Woodcock, *Anarchism,*

(London: Penguin, 1979) p. 144.

26. Clifford Harper's adaptation of Tristan Tzara, *1918 Dada Manifesto*, Clifford Harper, *Anarchy: A Graphic Guide,* (London: Camden Press, 1987) p. 195.

27. Emma Goldman, *My Further Disillusionment With Russia* (1924), in *The Anarchist Reader,* ed. by George Woodcock, (Glasgow: Fontana, 1986) p. 161.

28. Pierre-Joseph Proudhon, *Qu'est-ce que la Propriété* (1840) in *The Anarchist Reader,* ed. by George Woodcock, (Glasgow: Fontana, 1986) p. 71.

29. George Woodcock, *Herbert Read: The Stream and the Source,* (Montreal/New York/London: Black Rose Books, 2008) p. 234.

30. Andrew Harvey, *The Way of Passion: A Celebration of Rumi,* (New York: Jeremy P Tarcher/Putnam, 2001) p. 4.

31. Michael Bakunin, *Reaction in Germany*, cit. George Woodcock, *Anarchism,* (London: Penguin, 1979) p. 139.

32. Gustav Landauer, *For Socialism*, trans. by David J Parent, (St Louis: Telos Press, 1978), p. 26.

33. Herbert Read, *The Philosophy of Anarchism*, cit. Woodcock, *Herbert Read: The Stream and the Source,* p. 235.

34. Read, *The Philosophy of Anarchism* (1940) in *The Anarchist Reader,* p. 78.

35. Waterfield, p 123.

36. Meister Eckhart, cit. Waterfield, p. 121.

37. Martin Lings, *What is Sufism?,* (London: George Allen &Unwin Ltd, 1975) p. 94.

38. Nicholson, pp. 114-15.

39. René Guénon, *East and West*, trans. by Martin Lings, (Hillsdale NY: Sophia Perennis, 2004) p. 142.

IX

The Anarchist Paradox

1. George Woodcock, *Anarchism,* (London: Penguin, 1979) pp. 20-21.

2. Gustav Landauer, *For Socialism*, trans. by David J Parent, (St Louis: Telos Press, 1978) pp. 107-08.

3. George Woodcock, *Anarchism: A Historical Introduction*, in *The Anarchist Reader,* ed. by George Woodcock, (Glasgow: Fontana, 1986) p. 27.

4. Peter Marshall, *Demanding the Impossible: A History of Anarchism,* (London: Fontana Press, 1993) p. 15.

5. Michael Bakunin, *Federalism, Socialism and Anti-Theologism*, in *The Political Philosophy of Bakunin: Scientific Anarchism*, ed. by G.P. Maximoff, (New York: The Free Press of Glencoe, 1964) p. 59.

6. George Woodcock, *Herbert Read: The Stream and the Source,* (Montreal/New York/London: Black Rose Books, 2008) p. 4.

7. *Libellus XI (ii)*, in *Hermetica: The Ancient Greek and Latin Writings Which*

Contain Religious or Philosophical Teachings Ascribed to Hermes Trismegistus, ed. and trans. by Walter Scott, (Shaftesbury: Solos Press, 1997) p. 85.

8. Robin Waterfield, *René Guénon and The Future of the West: The life and writings of a 20th-century metaphysician,* (Wellingborough: Crucible, 1987) p.17.

9. Waterfield, p. 64.

10. Waterfield, p. 126.

11. Waterfield, p. 72.

12. Martin Lings, *What is Sufism?,* (London: George Allen & Unwin Ltd, 1975) p. 14.

13. CG Jung, *Psychology and Alchemy,* (London: Routledge, 1989) p. 148.

14. Karl Jaspers, *The Perennial Scope of Philosophy,* trans. by Ralph Manheim, (London: Routledge & Kegan Paul, 1950) p. 160.

15. Walter Scott, *Introduction, Hermetica: The Ancient Greek and Latin Writings Which Contain Religious or Philosophical Teachings Ascribed to Hermes Trismegistus,* p. 38.

16. Lings, p. 51.

17. Waterfield, p. 113.

18. Margaret Smith, *The Way of the Mystics: The Early Christian Mystics and the Rise of the Sufis,* (London: Sheldon Press, 1976) p. 3.

19. DC Lau, *Introduction,* Lao Tzu, *Tao Te Ching,* trans. by DC Lau, (London: Penguin, 1963) p.19.

20. *Notes from the Commentary of 'Abdul-Karim Jili,* Ibn 'Arabi, *Journey to the Lord of Power,* (London and The Hague: East West Publications, 1981) p. 70.

21. Marion Woodman and Elinor Dickson, *Dancing In the Flames: The Dark Goddess in the Transformation of Consciousness,* (Boston: Shambhala, 1997) p. 211.

22. Jaspers, *The Perennial Scope of Philosophy,* p. 98.

23. Waterfield, p.76.

24. Jaspers, *The Perennial Scope of Philosophy,* p. 39.

25. Waterfield, p. 128.

X

The Poetry of Revolt

1. Max Cafard, *Nietzschean Anarchy and the Post-Mortem Condition* in *I Am Not A Man, I Am Dynamite: Friedrich Nietzsche and the Anarchist Tradition,* ed. by John Moore with Spencer Sunshine, (Brooklyn, New York: Autonomedia, 2004) p. 90.

2. Frithjof Schuon, *The Transcendent Unity of Religions,* trans. by Peter Townsend, (London: Faber & Faber, 1953) p. 27.

3. Herbert Read, *The Philosophy of Anarchism* (1940) in *The Anarchist Reader,* ed. by George Woodcock, (Glasgow: Fontana, 1986) p. 74.

4. Herbert Read, *The Contrary Experience*, cit. George Woodcock, *Herbert Read: The Stream and the Source,* (Montreal/New York/London: Black Rose Books, 2008) p. 215.

5. Gustav Landauer, *For Socialism*, trans. by David J Parent, (St Louis: Telos Press, 1978) p. 54.

6. Russell Berman and Tim Luke, *Introduction*, Landauer, *For Socialism*, p. 7.

7. Read, cit. Woodcock, *Herbert Read: The Stream and the Source,* p. 206.

8. Herbert Read, *Phases of English Poetry*, cit. Woodcock, *Herbert Read: The Stream and the Source,* p. 70.

9. CG Jung, *Modern Man in Search of a Soul,* (London: Routledge & Kegan, 1978) p. 195.

10. Berman and Luke, *Introduction*, Landauer, *For Socialism*, pp. 8-9.

11. Jung, *Modern Man in Search of a Soul,* p. 194.

12. Oswald Spengler, *The Decline of the West,* (Oxford: Oxford University Press, 1991) p. 157.

13. John Ruskin, *The Mysteries of Life and Its Arts*, in *The Genius of John Ruskin: Selections from his Writings,* ed. by John D Rosenberg, (London, George Allen & Unwin Ltd, 1964) p. 343.

14. Andrew Harvey, *The Way of Passion: A Celebration of Rumi,* (New York: Jeremy P Tarcher/Putnam, 2001) p. 2.

15. Harvey, p. 166.

16. Robin Waterfield, *René Guénon and The Future of the West: The life and writings of a 20th-century metaphysician,* (Wellingborough: Crucible, 1987) p. 114.

17. CG Jung, *Psychology and Alchemy,* (London: Routledge, 1989) p. 481.

18. Gustav Landauer, *Revolution and Other Writings: A Political Reader,* ed. and trans. by Gabriel Kuhn, (Oakland: PM Press, 2010) p. 170.

19. Herbert Read, *The Forms of Things Unknown,* cit. Woodcock, *Herbert Read: The Stream and the Source,* p. 204.

20. Herbert Marcuse, *One Dimensional Man: Studies in the Ideology of Advanced Industrial Society,* (London: Routledge & Kegan Paul, 1964), p. 252.

21. Marcuse, pp. 245-46.

22. Marcuse, p. 246.

23. Waterfield, p. 78.

24. Waterfield, p. 142.

25. Idries Shah, *The Sufis,* (London: WH Allen & Co, 1977) p. 121.

26. Waterfield, p. 72.

XI

¡Viva la Revelación!

1. Oswald Spengler, *The Decline of the West,* (Oxford: Oxford University Press, 1991) pp. 324-25.

2. Karl Jaspers, *The Perennial Scope of Philosophy*, trans. by Ralph Manheim, (London: Routledge & Kegan Paul, 1950) p. 107.

3. Saul Newman, *Anarchism and the Politics of Ressentiment* in *I Am Not A Man, I Am Dynamite: Friedrich Nietzsche and the Anarchist Tradition,* ed. by John Moore with Spencer Sunshine, (Brooklyn, New York: Autonomedia, 2004) p. 122.

4. Jaspers, *The Perennial Scope of Philosophy*, p. 107.

5. Frithjof Schuon, *The Transcendent Unity of Religions,* trans. by Peter Townsend, (London: Faber & Faber, 1953) pp. 115-16.

6. Martin Lings, *What is Sufism?*, (London: George Allen Unwin Ltd, 1975) p. 23.

7. Leo Tolstoy, *A Calendar of Wisdom,* (London: Hodder & Stoughton, 1998) p. 243.

8. Gustav Landauer, *For Socialism*, trans. by David J Parent, (St Louis: Telos Press, 1978) p. 82 & p. 130.

9. CG Jung, *Modern Man In Search of A Soul,* (London: Routledge & Kegan Paul, 1978) p. 282.

10. Derrick Jensen, *Dreams,* (New York: Seven Stories Press, 2011) p. 444.

11. *Ascelpius III,* in *Hermetica: The Ancient Greek and Latin Writings Which Contain Religious or Philosophical Teachings Ascribed to Hermes Trismegistus,* ed. and trans. by Walter Scott, (Shaftesbury: Solos Press, 1997) p. 128.

ABOUT THE AUTHOR

Paul Cudenec is a writer, poet and activist living in the south of England. His previous writing includes *Antibodies: Life, Death and Resistance in the Psyche of the Superorganism* and *We Anarchangels of Creative Destruction*. For more information and contact details visit paulcudenec.blogspot.co.uk

27305090R00085

Printed in Great Britain
by Amazon